GW00370485

Student Life: A Survival Guide

Natasha Roe

Student Helpbook Series

Lifetime Careers

Student Life: A Survival Guide – third edition

This edition revised May 2002

Published by Lifetime Careers Publishing, 7 Ascot Court, White Horse Business Park, Trowbridge BA14 0XA

© Lifetime Careers Wiltshire Ltd, 2002

ISBN 1 902876 36 9

Printed and bound by Cromwell Press Ltd, Trowbridge

Cover design by Jane Norman

Cartoons for all books in the Student Helpbook Series by Mark Cripps

Acknowledgements

All anecdotes were researched and compiled by Isabelle Brewerton, fourth-year modern and medieval languages student, Corpus Christi College, Cambridge University.

With thanks to the following students and graduates who have contributed their experience and advice:

Phil Agulnik, Claire Baldwin, Paul Blundell, Isabelle Brewerton, Andy Bridges, Sarah Brown, Cherry Canovan, Jeremy Carlton, Sukanta Chowdhury, Jonathan Clayton, Mona Lisa Cook, Susanna Craig, Elizabeth Hardaker, Jennifer Hogan, Katie Hogan, Deborah Hyde, Allan Jones, Rhian Jones, Natalie King, Katherine Lawrey, Alastair Lee, Tony Leighton, Rob Lucas, Phil Marsh, Rhiannon Michael, Phil Mitchel, Andrew Newsome, Amy North, Samantha Northey, Phil Pearce, Martin Petchey, Anna Roberts, Peter Rodger, Vicky Spencer, Andrew Stephenson, Amanda Warburton, Lindsey Wilson, William Wilson, Katrina Woods.

With additional thanks to Alec Leggat.

Please note: You'll find that the term 'university' has been used throughout this book as shorthand for 'university or college/institute of higher education'.

Contents

How? Why? What? When? Where? Who?

You know where you are going to study and where you are going to study it, but what about everything else? How are you going to get to university and where will you live? Who's going to pay all the bills and keep the landlord happy? What will the other students be like and how are you going to stay healthy? How are you going to make your student loan stretch while trying to get the most out of university life? And are you going to plunge headlong into the social swim or slip quietly into the library?

'It was a bit of a culture shock starting university. On the first day when your parents leave you in your room, with all your stuff just dumped there, it takes a while to sink in. But then you meet other people and talk to them, which takes your mind off things. And the comforting thing is that everybody else is in the same situation.'

Phil Pearce, fifth-year business studies student, Luton University

Student Life has the facts to answer your Frequently Asked Questions. Don't be flummoxed about finding a flat, mystified by money, stumped about which sport to play, get into a quandary about qualifications or agonise over access. Next time you ask How? Why? What? When? Where? Who? just turn to *Student Life: A Survival Guide.*

Chapter 1
Money, money, money

You've probably thought hard about how you're going to manage your finances. But how much can you borrow and how can you make it stretch? Will you have to pay your tuition fees up front? And what about when you graduate? Will you have to start paying your loans and debts off immediately?

Student funding has undergone dramatic changes. Recent legislation has altered the money available to students and the contributions they're expected to make and in 2001 the government announced that they were going to review the system again so you'll need to check for the latest information. We've included contact details and websites of organisations who can tell you more throughout this chapter and in the *Lifesavers* section at the end.

'The main money problems I have had have always been as I reach the end of each term because the loan cheques come in at the beginning of each term, pretty much. Don't think that you have loads of money at the start of term because by the end of term those things that you bought when you thought you had loads of money will really annoy you!'

**Elizabeth Hardaker, fourth-year biology masters student,
University of Bath**

This chapter tells you what money is currently available to students, provides advice on how to make sure you get all you're entitled to and gives you tips on how to make the pennies stretch further. However, because each student's grant entitlement and tuition fees contribution are assessed on an individual basis, always consult the grants department of the council where you live, your local education authority (LEA), for the rules and regulations that apply to you. It's listed in the phone book under the name of your local council. Scottish students need to consult the Student Awards Agency for Scotland, while Northern Irish students should contact their local Education and Library Board (ELB). See the *Lifesavers* section for details.

There are two main sources of financial support to English, Welsh and Northern Irish students:

○ an assessed contribution to the tuition fees you are liable for

○ a student loan, part of which is assessed on your family income (means-tested).

For students who live and study in Scotland there are three main sources of financial support:

○ full contribution to tuition fees, regardless of your family income

○ a young student's bursary, a grant that is assessed on your family income (means-tested)

○ a student loan, most of which is assessed on your family income (means-tested).

Will I have to pay tuition fees?

English and Welsh students have to contribute towards their tuition fees if their residual family income (your LEA calculates this, based on your family's income before tax, taking off allowances for things like adult dependants) exceeds around £20,500. Below £20,500 the government will pay all tuition fees. The amount of tuition fees you're expected to pay is assessed on a sliding scale up to a maximum of £1,100 for the academic year 2002/2003. You will have to pay tuition fees for each year of your course and the amount you have to contribute has risen each year in line with inflation since 1998, when they were first introduced. (See also *What is taken into account during means-testing?*, page 17.)

You do not have to pay fees for certain health professional and postgraduate teacher training courses. (See also *What support is available to students on NHS-funded courses?*, page 22.)

What about tuition fees in Scotland?

Scottish students who study at Scottish universities don't have to make any contribution towards their tuition fees, regardless of their family's income. However, Scottish students studying at universities elsewhere in the UK will be assessed for contributions towards their tuition fees, as will students from other parts of the UK who study at Scottish universities.

'I knew that I wouldn't have to pay tuition fees because of my parents' low income but I don't know anyone, as far as I'm aware, who chose Scotland because you don't pay tuition fees.'

Lindsey Wilson, third-year psychology student, Edinburgh University

What about tuition fees in Northern Ireland?

Northern Irish students are assessed in a similar way to English and Welsh students, unless they live in Northern Ireland and study at a college in the Republic of Ireland, in which case the Irish government will pay all tuition fees.

Who will assess how much of my tuition fees I have to pay?

Your local education authority (LEA) or Education and Library Board (ELB) in Northern Ireland can tell you before you start your course how much of your tuition fees the government will pay and how much you need to pay. You need to apply to your LEA or ELB each year to get their contribution to your tuition fees.

When will I have to pay tuition fees?

Your university is responsible for charging you for your tuition fees and collecting payment. It's up to them when they ask you to pay your fees and there's no set 'plan' so it will differ from one university to another. Tuition fees can't be paid after graduation – they have to be paid up front when the university asks for them. However, the government has encouraged universities to ask for tuition fees in instalments, so you may not have to fork out all the money at once.

If you don't pay then it's up to the university what they do but it could result in you having to leave your course.

What are student loans?

Student loans are the main source of money available to students. 75% of the student loan is available to all eligible students but whether you can take out the other 25% will depend on your income or that of your parents, spouse or long-term partner. You can take out a student loan for each year of your course. You have to pay back the full amount of all the loans you take out. You start repaying your loans once you finish your degree and start earning over £10,000, though this figure is reviewed annually. The repayments will include interest payments which are linked to the rate of inflation, so that what you pay back is worth the same as the amount that you borrowed.

'A good idea is to put your student loan into a savings account when you first get it, which is something I wish I had done.'

**Jeremy Carlton, PhD biochemistry student,
Bristol University**

For English, Welsh and Northern Irish students the loan rates for 2002/2003 are as follows. These rates are adjusted each year in line with inflation. The amount of loan available in the final year is reduced, reflecting the fact that the academic year is shorter.

Student loan rates 2002/2003

Full year

	Maximum loan	Amount that is means-tested
Living at parental home, London or elsewhere	£3,090	£770
Living away from home, studying outside London	£3,905	£975
Living away from home, studying in London	£4,815	£1,205

Final year

	Maximum loan	Amount that is means-tested
Living at parental home, London or elsewhere	£2,700	£680
Living away from home, studying outside London	£3,390	£845
Living away from home, studying in London	£4,175	£1,045

What about funding for Scottish students?

Scotland also has a partially means-tested loans system but the amount that is means-tested for Scottish students is different from other parts of the UK, reflecting the difference in tuition fee contributions and the availability of the young student's bursary.

Scottish student loan rates 2002/2003

Full year

	Maximum loan	Amount that is means-tested
Living at home, studying in Scotland	£3,090	£2,580
Living away from home, studying in Scotland	£3,905	£3,135
Living in parental home, studying outside Scotland and London	£3,090	£1,480
Living elsewhere, studying outside Scotland and London	£3,905	£2,035
Living elsewhere, studying in London	£4,815	£2,800

Final year

	Maximum loan	Amount that is means-tested
Living at home, studying in Scotland	£2,700	£2,290
Living away from home, studying in Scotland	£3,390	£2,725
Living in parental home, studying outside Scotland and London	£2,700	£1,190
Living elsewhere, studying outside Scotland and London	£3,390	£1,625
Living elsewhere, studying in London	£4,175	£2,280

There is an additional loan of £510 available to some young students from families with an income of below £18,400. If you are eligible, then this will automatically be added to your loan when you apply. It applies to both students studying in Scotland and outside.

Young student's bursary

Scottish students who live and study in Scotland can also apply for a young student's bursary, which is a means-tested grant that doesn't have to be paid back at the end of the course. Students with parents who earn £10,000 or below can get the maximum grant of £2,050. The amount of grant available is then assessed on a sliding scale, tapering to £1,000 at £16,000 and zero at £26,200. You need to apply to the Student Awards Agency Scotland for this at the same time as you apply for your tuition fees and loan assessment.

Travel expenses

Means-tested travelling expenses are available of up to £465 plus £3 per day for unmarried students living at home and £635 plus £3 per day for married students living in their own home. Students living away from their home can claim the cost of three return journeys from their term-time residence to their home, plus up to £3 per day. Travel expenses need to be claimed separately on form AB4 at the end of January and no later than 31 July of the academic year to which they relate.

Graduate endowment

From 2001 Scottish students who study at a Scottish university have to pay a graduate endowment, currently £2,000, when they graduate. This can either be paid as a lump sum or through a specially arranged student loan which will then be repaid under the standard student loan system.

When is my loan paid?

Your loan will be paid in termly instalments and the first cheque should be ready for you when you arrive at university, providing you have filled out all the forms correctly.

'Loans don't provide enough money and I don't like the fact that we have to pay them back. I feel it is unfair that the government has changed the system because it means that it is more difficult for some students to leave home and so they can't have the full university experience. In my case I am away from home but you still can't enjoy the full experience because you are constantly counting your pennies.'

Jonathan Clayton, third-year biochemistry student,
UMIST

When do I start paying my loan back?

You don't start paying your loan back until you've left your course and started earning. Current students have to pay their loans back once they start earning £10,000 a year, although this threshold is reviewed annually. The amount you pay back each month is worked out as a percentage of your monthly income. This is currently 9% of your income. So a graduate earning £12,000 a year will pay £15 a month, while a graduate earning £17,000 will make monthly payments of £52. If your income drops to below £10,000 then you stop making repayments and if you never earn £10,000 per year you never make any repayments. There's no time limit by which you have to repay your loan but you owe interest on your loan, which is linked to the rate of inflation, from the time you leave college.

The Student Loans Company and Inland Revenue work together to collect payments. If you work for an employer then your loan repayments will be taken out of your salary through the Pay As You Earn scheme.

Which students are eligible for financial support?

To be able to apply for a contribution towards your tuition fees and a student loan you must have lived in the UK for three years before the start of your course or be an overseas student with no restrictions about how long you can stay in the UK. There are exemptions for some students, including those from EU countries, so check with your LEA, ELB or the Student Awards Agency for Scotland if you are unsure about whether you qualify. And while there are no age restrictions on those that can apply for tuition fee contributions, students wanting to apply for loans must be under 50 (or under 55 providing they undertake to return to employment at the end of their course).

You must also be attending a course that is eligible. The main ones are first degree courses, HND, HNC courses in medical, veterinary, dental and science subjects, Diploma of Higher Education courses or Initial Teacher Training or PGCE courses. If you are unsure, check as the government is considering widening the number of courses that are eligible.

What is taken into account during means testing?

Your income will be taken into account automatically and also that of:

○ your parents if you are not independent (see below)

○ your spouse or long-term partner if you are over 25 and are in a stable relationship with a heterosexual partner.

Your parents' income is not taken into account if you are judged to be an 'independent' student. This applies if:

○ you are 25 or over by the time that you start your course

○ you are under 25 but are married

○ you have been supporting yourself for three years before your course begins

○ you are estranged from your parents or have been in care.

'As a mature student I don't qualify for any financial help from my Local Education Authority, nor am I sponsored by my employer. To do my course, I had to start working part-time, which meant moving back home with my parents – not easy at the age of 35! My advice is to ask, ask, ask about every hardship loan, bursary or scholarship there is going!'

Deborah Hyde, first-year history student, Birkbeck College, University of London

---

How do I apply for financial support?

To apply for assistance with tuition fee payments, for student loans or for other help you might be entitled to (such as additional support for disabled students or those with children) you need to apply to your local education authority (LEA) in England and Wales, Education and Library Board (ELB) in Northern Ireland or Student Awards Agency for Scotland – depending on where you live. You should apply in the January or February of the year in which you hope to go to university.

Return the application form by the deadline you are given and you will be told whether you are eligible for support and sent a financial form to complete. You need to fill this out and return it by the deadline, after which you will be sent a financial notification form and a student loan request form. You'll need to complete the student loan request form and send it to the Student Loans Company (see *Lifesavers*). The sooner you do this the better the chances of your first loan instalment being ready for you to collect when you get to university.

Is there extra money I can claim?

There are certain circumstances under which you're able to claim additional allowances. You can take out additional student loans if:

○ you're required to study for longer than 30 weeks and three days or if you have to go abroad as part of your course

○ you have dependants or are a single parent

○ you are under 21 but have been in care since you were 16

○ you have extra travel costs to meet.

Can my university or college help with funding?

The government gives universities some funds to help students who have particular financial difficulties. These are administered through the universities and include:

O **hardship funds**, usually only of a few hundred pounds, for UK students following degree courses who get into financial difficulties. It's sometimes worth applying towards the end of the academic year in case your university hasn't used up all its hardship fund money

O **hardship loans** for students in severe financial difficulties. You have to apply through your university and then repay it through the student loans system. Again, these usually only run to a few hundred pounds

O **opportunity bursaries** for students under 21 who come from low-income families

O **access bursaries** for students with dependants

O **mature students bursaries** for students with children who are not eligible for the new childcare grant.

For all these, you need to check that you meet the criteria. You also need to apply directly to your university.

What additional help can disabled students claim?

'I knew about the money I could claim under the disabled students' allowance but I found out about an access report quite late. This is a report carried out by a college attached to the Royal National Institute for the Blind (RNIB) where an assessor assesses your personal requirements. However, it later transpired that my college didn't act on this report and I had a great deal of difficulty getting the resources I needed and, in most cases, didn't get them. I felt that there was a certain disbelief on the part of the college that these resources were available.'

Tony Leighton, theology and philosophy of religion student,
Oxford University

If you have a disability or specific learning difficulty, like dyslexia, you may be able to claim for additional funds from your LEA, ELB or

19

the Student Awards Agency for Scotland. Known as the disabled students' allowance, it is intended to meet the extra costs of studying that you incur because of your disability. It's not intended to meet the disability-related costs you have whether you study or not. Unlike tuition fees contributions and student loans, it's not means-tested, so neither your, nor your parents' or spouse's, income will be taken into account.

There are three areas you can claim under.

- **General allowance** – Currently up to £1,455 a year, this is intended to meet any additional study costs you have because of your disability. For instance, you may require typing or transcription services.

- **Specialist equipment allowance** – A one-off payment, currently up to £4,355, which can be used, for example, to buy computer equipment, Braille equipment or a portable induction loop.

- **Non-medical personal helper allowance** – Money, up to a total of £11,015 a year which can be used to help you fully participate in university life. You can use it to pay for a sign-language interpreter, someone to take your notes or to help you to travel around the university.

'I have dyslexia and in my first year my university helped me apply to my LEA and I got a computer out of it!'

**Claire Baldwin, third-year history student,
Aberystwyth University**

You need to provide to your assessment authority medical proof of your disability from a doctor, audiologist, educational psychologist or specialist dyslexia teacher. If you haven't been assessed in the last two years then your LEA, ELB or the Student Awards Agency for Scotland may need a new assessment, for which you may have to pay.

Benefits

Some disabled students are able to claim income support, housing benefit and other benefits, to cover additional costs. You have to meet certain criteria to qualify for these benefits, so contact Skill or a local independent advice organisation such as the Citizens' Advice Bureau (see *Lifesavers*) before you fill out any claim forms.

More information and advice about financial support while you are studying can be found by contacting:

Skill: National Bureau for Students with Disabilities – *Chapter House, 18–20 Crucifix Lane, London SE1 3JW. Tel/text phone: 020 7450 0620, 0800 328 5050 (information service). www.skill.org.uk*

Skill in Northern Ireland: National Bureau for Students with Disabilities – *Unit 2, Jennymount Court, North Derby Street, Belfast BT15 3HN. Tel/text phone: 028 9028 7000.*

Skill in Scotland: National Bureau for Students with Disabilities – *Norton Park, 57 Albion Road, Edinburgh EH7 5QY. Tel/text phone: 0131 457 2348.*

Or you can get hold of the annual publication *Bridging the Gap: A Guide to the Disabled Students' Allowances in Higher Education* by calling 0800 731 9133 or 0800 216 280 (text phone) or you can download it from www.dfes.gov.uk/studentsupport/student_disabled.cfm

Can I get extra funding if part of my course involves studying abroad?

If you are on a full-time course or part-time Initial Teacher Training (ITT) course lasting more than six weeks and have to study overseas for at least eight weeks as a mandatory part of your course, you are entitled to a higher rate of loan, depending on the classification of the country. Full-time paid sandwich-year students, those receiving NHS bursaries and ITT students on courses of less than six weeks are entitled to reduced overseas studies loan rates. Ask your assessment authority for details.

Loan rates for overseas study 2002/2003

Full year

Higher cost countries	£5,670 of which	£1,420 is means-tested
High cost countries	£4,770 of which	£1,190 is means-tested
Other countries	£3,905 of which	£975 is means-tested

Final year

Higher cost countries	£4,935 of which	£1,235 is means-tested
High cost countries	£4,150 of which	£1,035 is means-tested
Other countries	£3,390 of which	£845 is means-tested

Higher cost countries: Denmark, Hong Kong, Japan, Switzerland, Taiwan.

High cost countries: Australia, Austria, Belgium, Commonwealth of Independent States, Finland, France, Germany, Iceland, Indonesia, Eire, Israel, Italy, Luxembourg, Netherlands, New Zealand, Norway, Republic of Korea, Sweden, USA.

21

What support is available to students on NHS-funded courses?

Students who are awarded NHS-funded places on full-time, part-time or pre-registration courses can apply for support under the NHS bursary scheme. There's a means-tested bursary scheme and a non-means-tested scheme but whatever bursary you are awarded you will not have to pay it back, nor will you have to make a contribution towards tuition fees. And from September 2002 the NHS pre-registration bursary scheme will be extended to cover the tuition fees of medical and dental students from the fifth year of their courses.

Means-tested bursaries are available in England for students following NHS-funded courses in areas such as chiropody, physiotheraphy, dietetics, radiography, speech and language therapy, courses allied to the dental profession - such as dental hygiene, and degree-level courses in nursing and midwifery. The rules are broadly similar for students studying in Wales, Northern Ireland and Scotland but you need to check with the relevant authority (see below).

Students eligible for a means-tested bursary can also take out a lower rate of student loan, part of which will also be means-tested, through the Student Loan Company (see *Lifesavers*).

Non-means-tested bursaries are available to students studying for nursing and midwifery diploma courses. Loans are not available to students awarded a non means-tested bursary.

Students who have been given an NHS-funded place should find out about the bursary support available to them by contacting the relevant organisation. Check with your institution that your place is NHS-funded.

England: NHS Student Grants Unit – *Room 212c, Government Buildings, Norcross, Blackpool FY5 3TA. Tel: 01253 655655.*

Northern Ireland: Department for Employment and Learning – *Student Support Branch, 4ᵗʰ Floor, Adelaide House, 39–49 Adelaide Street, Belfast BT2 8FD. Tel: 028 9025 7777.*

Scotland: Student Awards Agency for Scotland – *3 Redheughs Rigg, South Gyle, Edinburgh EH12 9HH. Tel: 0131 476 8212.*

Wales: The NHS (Welsh) Student Awards Unit – *2ⁿᵈ Floor, Golgate House, 101 St Mary Street, Cardiff CF10 1DX. Tel: 029 2026 1495.*

There's also more information about NHS bursaries in a Department of Health publication, *Financial Help for Health Care Students,* which you can get by contacting:

Department of Health – *PO Box 777, London SE1 6XH.*
www.doh.gov.uk/hcsmain.htm

Alternatively, you could call NHS Careers for information on 0845 60 60 655.

What extra help is available to mature students?

The 1999 Hardship Survey carried out by the National Union of Students found that mature students had substantially more debt than other students as they often needed more money because of greater commitments, or had existing debts. So you need to make sure you investigate everything that you might be entitled to. Depending on your particular circumstances, you may be able to get help with tuition fees, childcare costs, grants for dependants or travel and equipment costs, some of which won't affect any benefits you might be claiming. Some mature students may also be eligible for a maximum £500 non-repayable means-tested access bursary. However, if you are over 25 and are married or living in a stable heterosexual relationship then your income, or that of your partner, will be assessed. Ask your university, local education authority, Library and Education Board or the Student Awards Agency for Scotland for details, or try *Coming Back to Learning* by Monica Brand et al. (Lifetime Careers Publishing, £10.99) or *Mature Students' Guide: Getting into Higher Education for 21 Plus* by Liz Maynard and Simon Pearsall (Trotman, £9.99).

What help is available to part-time students?

If you are studying part-time then you can apply for help with your tuition fees and for a student loan. Loans for part-time students are £500 a year and you can apply for a maximum of six loans. Application packs are available from the **Department for Education and Skills** information line on 0800 731 9133 or www.dfes.gov.uk/studentsupport

What if I am studying to be a teacher?

Students who are studying for the Postgraduate Certificate in Education (PGCE) don't have to pay tuition fees. There are also additional financial incentives for those following postgraduate Initial Teacher Training (ITT) courses although these don't apply to students from Northern Ireland. For further information on teacher training programmes call the teacher information line on 0845 6000 991 or for Welsh speakers on 0845 6000 992 or visit the **Teacher Training Agency's** website at www.canteach.gov.uk or find information at www.teachernet.gov.uk

What about dance and drama students?

The only source of public financial support available to dance and drama students taking approved professional courses at privately funded schools is the Dance and Drama Awards Scheme. Under this scheme 820 students following approved courses at participating schools can be assessed for a tuition fees contribution (up to a maximum of £1,100 for 2002/2003) and for help with maintenance (living and learning) costs. Call 0114 259 3612 for information.

Other dance and drama students who do not qualify for a Dance and Drama Award should see *What if I am not able to claim financial support?* below, *Could I be sponsored?*, page 25 and *Can I get extra money through scholarships?*, page 27.

What if I am not able to claim financial support?

If you study at a privately-funded college and do not qualify for financial support from your local education authority then you may be able to apply for a Career Development Loan. They are designed to cover course fees, books, materials and living expenses for both part-time and full-time courses, although you need to be studying a vocational course (i.e. one that gives you practical skills that will lead to employment). To find out more call 0800 585 505 or visit www.lifelonglearning.co.uk/cdl

See also the Educational Grants Advisory Service in the *Lifesavers* section at the end of this chapter.

Could I be sponsored?

Some companies sponsor students through university and pay them to work during the holidays. You stand a much better chance of being given sponsorship if you plan to study pure or applied science, or engineering. However, business and commerce-related subjects, such as economics, banking and accountancy, can all attract sponsorship. Although there's not usually a formal arrangement, sponsored students are often offered a job at the end of their degree. You can also be sponsored through a 'student apprenticeship' scheme where you're employed by a company which offers you a combination of in-house training and higher education courses. Apply well in advance and be prepared to write to many companies before you find one which is interested in you.

'I did a 12-month placement in my third year. I had to find my own placement, apply and go for interview like for any job. I have to wait an extra year before I get my degree but personally I think it's good to have a year's work experience, it makes you more competitive in the job market. Also you are paid, which means that you can pay off some of the debts you've made in the first two years!'

William Wilson, fourth-year management student,
Aston University

You can be sponsored for either a full-time or a sandwich course. In fact, sandwich courses lend themselves particularly well to sponsorship, as part of the course requirement is that you spend some time in industry and you can usually arrange to do this with the firm that sponsors you. This is traditionally done under a 3:1 ratio (where you spend three years following a course of higher education and one year in industry) and this structure is well established in some universities. However, many sponsored students follow sandwich courses of a different structure or arrange to do any work as part of the sponsorship deal during the vacations.

Some sponsors will offer you sponsorship after you have started your degree, maybe following a period of work experience or because your university has good ties with local employers.

There can be disadvantages to being sponsored. Some companies require you to follow a particular course, so consider whether this is right for you, without being swayed too much by the prospect of extra cash. Find out how flexible or specific the courses or training schemes are and make the right selection for you. It is also important to find out whether you'll be bound to the company after you've completed your course.

If you're a humanities student then sponsorship is probably not an option unless you have very strong contacts with a large company. But don't be afraid to ask. The worst that can happen is that they say no.

Some universities have sponsorship officers who can tell you more and help to find a company to sponsor you. If yours doesn't then you can find information about companies that sponsor students at your local careers office (listed in the phone book under 'careers').

There are also publications which tell you more about sponsorship and list potential sponsors. *A Question of Sponsorship?* a free leaflet from the Student Sponsorship Information Services (SSIS), PO Box 36, Newton-Le-Willows, Merseyside WA12 ODW; *Sponsorship and Funding Directory 2003*, published by CRAC/Hobsons which lists over 2,500 sponsorship opportunities at £8.99 + £1.50 p&p from Plymbridge Distributors Ltd (0870 900 2665) and the *Educational Grants Directory 2002/2003* by Sarah Harland and Dave Griffiths, £21.95, also available from Plymbridge Distributors Ltd.

'When I was on placement I still had a few money worries because as a student I was paid a lot less than the other people that I worked with but they didn't realise this and expected me to be able to spend as much as them when we hung out. So if you are expecting to save a huge amount of money on placement you probably won't!'

Elizabeth Hardaker, fourth-year biology masters student, University of Bath

The Army, Navy and Air Force also offer sponsorship for higher education courses under two different schemes – bursaries and cadetships. Bursaries are given to students interested in the armed forces but who don't want to commit themselves to a career in the forces immediately. Cadetships mean you join one of the armed forces and are paid a salary while at university. Under both schemes you have to attend training sessions at weekends, for which you'll be paid. The amount of time you have to serve in the force which has sponsored you varies according to whether you're awarded a cadetship or a bursary.

As with other forms of sponsorship, the Forces tend to give preference to scientific and engineering courses, although subjects such as dentistry, medicine and catering are also considered. The emphasis is on your commitment to the Forces, so even if you're studying languages or other humanities subjects your application may be considered. For more information contact your nearest Armed Forces careers office (listed in the phone book). Alternatively, there's information at www.army.mod.uk; www.raf-careers.com and www.royal-navy.mod.uk

---

'I was sponsored by DERA which is an agency of the Ministry of Defence – they do research and development work and have had numerous name changes. They basically gave me money to tell people who they were. There was an option to work for them but I never did as it wasn't the area I was interested in. I did it purely for the money. I would recommend it to others but it's rare to get such an easy deal as mine. I suggest that you keep your eyes open for opportunities that may arise – it's often a question of luck.'

Sarah Brown, maths graduate,
Christ's College, Cambridge University

Can I get extra money through scholarships?

Some universities and professional institutions offer scholarships in certain subjects to particularly gifted students who may also have to fulfil other criteria such as academic background or residency requirements. Scholarships differ from sponsorship in that there are not usually any work commitments included and they can be awarded in a variety of fields like sports, arts, music, and science. However, scholarships are usually oversubscribed and are likely to involve extra interviews and exams, though you won't have to pay them back. So if you are interested in finding out more then ask your university about its scholarships, visit www.scholarship-search.org.uk or get hold of a copy of *A Guide to University Scolarships and Awards* by Brian Heap for £14.99 plus £1.50 p&p from Plymbridge Distributors Ltd (0870 900 2665).

Can charities help?

Some charities provide funds for educational courses but you'll have to meet their very specific criteria. Some will only give funds to students who have already started a course and find they're not able to complete it because of a lack of money. If this is the case you have to prove that you've explored all other avenues of funding.

The amount you get is likely to be limited and unlikely to fund an entire course, although it's possible to approach several organisations. Research the charity thoroughly so you can present your case well. For more information about charities with educational trusts look in libraries for the *Charities Digest* and the *Directory of Grant-Making Trusts*.

Will I need to work?

Most students find they have to work while they are at university. You need to be careful about balancing work and study but you can use the need to work to build up your curriculum vitae (CV). The graduate job market is becoming more competitive as the number of graduates increases. Employers want evidence that you're interested in the job, or at least some signs of initiative, so anything you can do to improve your chances while at university is vital. See also *How do I get the most out of university life?*, page 95 and *Life after university*, Chapter 8.

> *'Get a job in the first and second years so that you don't have to work too much in the third year when you have less time.'*
>
> **Vicky Spencer, third-year textile design student, Chelsea College of Art and Design**

Can I work part-time while studying?

Be careful about taking on too much outside work during term time. It's possible to balance both but you need to be organised (see *Down to work*, Chapter 5). 30% of students who work during term time missed lectures because of their employment, according to a GMB/NUS survey.

> *'I worked at a One Stop convenience store part-time for a couple of years. I was the odd job man basically so there was usually something exciting to do such as scraping out the inside of a freezer or checking the deliveries. There were also the comedy moments of answering customers' questions like 'Do you sell wallpaper paste?' or 'Do you have any false fingernails?' whilst keeping a straight face.'*
>
> **Andy Bridges, third-year music technology and audio system design student, Derby University**

What part-time work is available will, to a large extent, depend on where you're studying. Your students' union will have information about local jobs and work within the union. Many students' unions actively provide as many jobs as possible for their students. It's usually bar, shop or security work but it can be the place where budding DJs get their first break. Alternatively, look in local newspapers, Jobcentres, employment agencies and on newsagents' noticeboards.

You can also try advertising your services. You may be able to use your degree subject to offer coaching and tuition or be paid for your babysitting, dog-walking, typing, domestic or DIY services. Local newsagents don't charge much to place advertisements in their windows and it's a good way of capturing the local market.

What about working during the vacations?

If possible, working during the holidays is a much better option as you'll leave yourself free to participate fully in undergraduate life and have a better chance of getting the sort of job that is a useful CV builder (see also *Life after university*, Chapter 8). However, there'll be masses of students all looking for employment during the vacations so try to get something sorted out well before term finishes and get a head start.

If you find it difficult to get work through Jobcentres and employment agencies try approaching anyone you've worked for before. Look out for seasonal opportunities too. The Post Office, for instance, employs extra workers during the Christmas period and there'll be seasonal fruit-picking and harvesting work in rural areas. Approach organisations involved in leisure industries, such as hotels, catering and sports centres, as these too have seasonal employment which fits in with student holidays. Try sending off speculative CVs to people who you think might be able to offer you work, ringing them up and even calling from door to door. Just think carefully about the skills you have to offer and then use your imagination to identify the people that can pay you for those skills.

To find out what jobs are available get hold of a copy of *Summer Jobs in Britain*, published annually, by the Vacation Work Publications or try local libraries.

Can I work abroad?

Working holidays can be very enjoyable and give you great experience but you probably won't earn much – usually just enough to keep you while you're there and perhaps enough to pay for your travel to the next destination. While working holidays are unlikely to bring a smile to your bank manager's face they're great for seeing the world on a tight budget and building up your CV. Student travel operators, your students' union or careers library will all have details of what is available. You can choose to do anything from fruit-picking and helping run children's camps to working on an archaeological dig. See also *Travelling around and staying safe*, Chapter 7.

There's a publication which details positions overseas called *Summer Jobs Abroad,* also available from the Directory of Social Change (020 7209 5157) or from libraries.

'I went to the US with Camp America. It was a great deal because they organise everything for you, providing you with a free flight and free accommodation. They also organise your visa for you. I was teaching tennis to kids. Camp America take a huge chunk of your salary but you get the rest. I only saved about £200. If you do it for a second year running then you end up with a lot more money. I met loads of people there, from all parts of the world.'

Phil Pearce, fifth-year business studies student,
Luton University

Can I find jobs on the web?

There are a great number of websites where you can find details of job vacancies for students. When applying for any job that you see advertised on the web, make sure that you are satisfied that it is genuine and being offered by a reputable employer before giving any personal details. Reputable employers should be quite happy to explain the opportunity to you before putting pressure on you to provide your details.

Here are some suggestions for websites where you can find details of vacancies for students, including part-time, vacation, seasonal and overseas jobs.

www.e4s.co.uk – employment for students site with term-time and holiday jobs, plus tips on enhancing your CV

www.hotrecruit.com – temporary and part-time jobs in the retail and fast-food industries

www.snapajob.com – site for 16- to 26-year-old students wanting to find term-time or seasonal jobs

www.summerjobs4students.com – an online directory of holiday jobs, vacation work, seasonal work and working holidays

www.totaljobs.com – very large site with temporary, part-time and graduate jobs listed

See also *Where are jobs advertised?*, Chapter 8.

Will I have to pay taxes?

As a full-time student you don't have to pay tax on any part-time or vacation work providing you don't earn more than the single person's allowance (£4,535 in 2001/2002). Tell your employer you're a student and he or she will give you a P38(S) to fill out. If you work abroad then read the guide *Going to Work Abroad* (1R58) which is available from your local tax office listed under Inland Revenue in the phone book.

Sandwich-year students will be taxed at the full rate but your placement will probably run either side of the tax year (April to March) so you may be able to claim some tax back when you finish. Final-year students will also be taxed at the normal rate for any work they do after they graduate. If you end up doing a series of temporary jobs and have not been working for the full financial year you should also be able to claim tax back.

If you have returned to education from employment then you may be able to claim back the additional tax you've paid while working as tax levels are set on the assumption you'll be working for the whole financial year. Get hold of form P50 and contact your local tax office if you need any help.

Find out more by reading IR60 *Income Tax and Students* available from your local tax office, listed under Inland Revenue in the phone book or visit www.inlandrevenue.gov.uk

What about National Insurance (NI)?

Most full-time students are not required to pay National Insurance contributions. However, if you have a job where you are earning over £87 per week then your employer will deduct National Insurance contributions from your salary. The amount they deduct will depend on your total earnings.

What do banks offer students?

Banks are interested in your earning potential once you graduate, so the competition for student accounts is very intense. All the large banks offer interest-free overdraft facilities to students so check out the terms and conditions and compare banks' overdraft offers. Remember to check the rate of interest charged if you go over your overdraft limit and look at the terms for graduates as you are unlikely to organise changing your bank as soon as you graduate. Compare the different offers at the **National Association for Managers of Student Services'** website at www.support4learning.org.uk/money/banks.htm

When choosing your bank you may also want to consider whether:

O there are any branches close to your university with cash-point machines

○ you get a cheque book and card

○ you can bank online

○ you are paid interest on current accounts

○ there are bank charges levelled on overdrafts once you graduate

○ you will be offered preferential rates for graduate loans.

'I've been with my bank for a long time so I decided to stick with them for customer loyalty I suppose. They have been very reasonable and set me up with an overdraft facility easily because I had used them during my year out and had a good account history. I recommend that if you have a good history with a bank, or used them while you've earned money on a year abroad, then stay with them. It can be tempting to swap banks because of student offers but there could be a sting in the tail later if they don't really know you and you need help.'

**Martin Petchey, second-year psychology student,
Luton University**

If you have a bank account at home which offers good student terms then there are arguments both for and against changing your branch. A university branch which is used to dealing with student accounts may be more sympathetic to students' needs but if you've a good record with your bank at home then it might make sense to stay with that branch. You can usually negotiate overdrafts over the phone and, if you do need to see your manager, you can do so in the holidays.

When you set up your account ask for monthly statements and check them thoroughly – banks do make mistakes. If you've made a note of every withdrawal and deposit, checking your statements should only take a few minutes.

How do I arrange an overdraft?

Always contact your bank before you go over the overdraft limit. Banks aren't impressed with people who assume they have access to money that isn't in their account and unarranged overdrafts are charged at a higher rate of interest than arranged ones. Phone up and be prepared to bargain, ideally having something to offer in return. This can be anything from a vacation job to your next loan cheque, providing it is not too far off.

Keep a record of how long your overdraft facility lasts and don't automatically assume it will be continued after this date just because you don't have the money to pay it back. You'll have to renegotiate your facility. If you need to extend your overdraft, contact your bank well in advance.

'I had trouble getting an overdraft at the beginning. I hassled the bank and eventually managed to sort it out by phoning them and saying that I had no money, that most students were allowed an overdraft limit and just kept arguing until they gave it to me. I don't know why they caused difficulties.'

Rob Lucas, third-year critical fine art practice student, Brighton University

What do banks charge for?

Bank charges are the fees that banks take out of your account to cover various transactions such as bounced cheques, letters and interest on overdrafts. They are standard charges but can seem very steep when you have so little money. The best way to avoid bank charges is to arrange everything properly and keep records of all correspondence. Banks are often willing to waive charges if you explain your situation in advance. If you find that you have been charged by mistake for something you have arranged in advance then ring at once, making sure you have all the proof you need, and you should get any charges reimbursed.

'I have got on very well with my bank. I have an overdraft facility which came automatically when I joined and it goes up by a small amount each year. They're always very helpful to me and I am very pleased with them.'

Katrina Woods, second-year sociology student, Ulster University

Should I have a credit card?

Be very careful about signing up for credit cards. The companies who offer credit cards don't have students in mind so the rates of interest will be far higher than your student loan or bank overdraft. They can also rapidly impose hefty penalties if you don't keep up with the payments. If you do take out a credit card then make sure you understand the terms and conditions and be careful about how you use it. If you are using your credit card to buy food then you should seek financial advice from your students' union or one of the groups listed in the *Lifesavers* section.

Avoid store cards and catalogue credits. The rates of interest are high, it's difficult to keep track of when you have to pay all the different accounts off by (even if you do have the money) and the punishments for non-payment are swift and severe.

How do I make the pennies stretch?

Don't be fooled by the relatively large sum of money deposited in your bank account at the beginning of term when you first receive your student loan cheque. When you break this down into weekly amounts and realise that it has to last you for the whole term, and possibly the vacation, all of a sudden it seems very small.

A Barclays' Graduate Survey in 2000 found that 85% of students interviewed were in debt and the average graduate debt is estimated to be £10,000. While this illustrates the point that you are going to have to watch your pennies, you are also more likely to earn more when you graduate (average starting salary currently around £15,000) and your chances of standing in the job seekers' queue are reduced by 50%.

'The important thing is to work out a budget and keep to it. You need to include extras. I am living in a house which means that I don't just have rent but bills as well, which can be a lot to pay in one go.'

Jonathan Clayton, third-year biochemistry student, UMIST

But budgeting is essential. Just look at the sample budgets below to see how tight money is. They are based on budgets drawn up by the National Union of Students (NUS) following their national hardship survey of students. They are based on the costs of two students, one studying in London and one elsewhere in the UK or Wales. You should use them as a guide only. Some things will vary according to whether you live at home and the type of books and equipment your course requires.

	Inside London	Outside London
Income		
Full student loan	4,815	3,905
Expenditure		
Tuition fees	1,100	1,100
Books/equipment, etc.	260	260

Photocopying	82	82
Rent	3,640	2,600
Utility bills	400	400
Food/household goods	1,300	1,100
Laundry	102	102
Insurance	95	95
Clothing	420	420
Travel	699	455
Entertainment	1,000	800
Total	**9,098**	**7,414**
Shortfall	**4,283**	**3,509**

While this is an example to illustrate the sorts of things you need to allocate money against, it also demonstrates how much money you need to find each year. Of course, you may not have to pay your tuition fees but even so most students nowadays find that they need to work during the vacations or part-time while they study, and use the overdraft facilities offered by banks. It also demonstrates the importance of working out your expenditure before you go wild.

'My main difficulties were with money, every student finds that. You realise how much everything costs – you have to pay for food, books, clothes, social life. It's hard to strike a balance, especially in the first year when you suddenly have the freedom to go out every night of the week. I think it's necessary to go through the overindulgence of the first year then you learn that you have to manage your finances. You have to weigh up your priorities.'

Samantha Northey, third-year Chinese student,
Edinburgh University

How do I stick to my budget?

Use these budgets as a template to work out what you need to budget for and allocate the money to rent, food, bills and travel before anything else. If you have any vacation or part-time work then remember to add your earnings to the income column. Once you've worked out what you need to spend on essentials then try to use your chequebook to pay for them, filling out the stubs each time. You'll find that you're not left with much for the non-essentials. Divide whatever this turns out to be into weekly amounts and only take this amount of money out of the cash-point each week.

'I wouldn't have had enough money without my parents' help. Any problems I did have were mostly my fault – like wasting money on take-aways and eating out instead of cooking myself. You can usually just use your common sense to find out how to save money.'

**Rob Lucas, third-year critical fine art practice student,
Brighton University**

However careful you are, you may find that there are times when the money isn't there to meet the essentials. Don't panic. Prioritise where the money has to go and talk to your bank manager. Your rent, food and travel are all vital but remember, if you don't pay the bills of the utility companies they'll cut you off and you'll be landed with an extra reconnection charge.

Never sit on unopened bills or ignore letters demanding money. Contact the people to whom you owe money immediately as they're often prepared to arrange other methods of payment. It's cheaper for them to allow you to pay over a period of time than to drag you through the courts. If you wait until things reach crisis point your finances will be much more difficult to sort out.

If you need help go to your students' union, the local Citizens' Advice Bureau or a debt counselling service *(see Lifesavers)*. You may also find some useful tips in *Balancing Your Books*, published by ECCTIS/CRAC, £5.99 or *A Student's Guide to Better Money Management* (£2) from Credit Action on 0800 591084.

Whatever you do, don't take out an unsecured loan. It's easy to get these loans but the rates of interest are crippling and you'll end up in even greater debt.

'Travelling is the main problem. It costs £50 a week to go by train because I live at home and I have to be in by 10 a.m., so I pay the peak travel rate.'

**Vicky Spencer, third-year textile design student,
Chelsea College of Art and Design**

Rent

Rent is the largest sum of money you have to find from your funds and it must be a priority. If you live in a hall of residence then pay your fees as soon as you get your grant or loan cheque. If you pay your rent right at the start then you won't have to worry about it again.

If you live in a privately rented house consider setting up a separate bank account for rent and bills. You can transfer the proportion of your loan cheque you need to cover this and not have to worry about finding the rent each month.

Groceries

'Eating cheaply is the main thing. Special offers are a great way of saving, especially when you buy as a group. I don't buy new clothes either.'

Jeremy Carlton, PhD biochemistry student,
Bristol University

If you live somewhere where it's easy to get fresh food from markets or local shops then it's better for you nutritionally, and for your pocket, if you buy food each day. If the only option you have is to shop in a supermarket, then buy food weekly, keeping your eyes open for 'multi-buy' or special offers. Write a weekly menu and buy only the ingredients you need. This reduces waste considerably. Buying in bulk and cooking in bulk also saves money, although you need to store the food properly. Try shopping late at night, especially on a Sunday, as many stores reduce prices dramatically on goods approaching their sell by dates. However, bear in mind that fruit or vegetables that aren't fresh have little nutritional value.

As a general rule of thumb always try to buy fruit and veg from markets, meat from butchers and fish from fishmongers. It's amazing how much cheaper food is when it isn't wrapped in plastic and the quality is often better. Always buy food that's in season – you can tell by looking at what's cheapest.

If you live in a shared house then it's cheaper to buy food as a household. This saves arguments about whose loaf of bread you're eating but doesn't work so well if some members of the household eat considerably more than others.

Avoid buying prepared and processed food. It's much more expensive and you can prepare your own, more nutritional meals in the same time (see *How do I eat healthily?*, page 83).

'Economy shopping is the main way to save money. Compare prices in the area and buy from the cheapest. Also, keep an eye out for bargains – 'buy-one-get-one-free' offers are really good for saving a lot of money.'

Allan Jones, third-year geography student,
Lancaster University

Bills

Utility companies all offer a variety of payment schemes. Choose the one that suits you best and is easiest to manage. Direct debit schemes mean that you don't have to worry about posting bills on time but this can be difficult to organise if you live in a shared house. Contact the utility companies for details of the payment schemes they run, choose the one that best suits all house members and read *Living on your own*, Chapter 3.

'Simple things can help, like remembering to turn the lights off when you leave a room and putting an extra jumper on instead of turning on the heating. It's all a question of making the effort.'

Allan Jones, third-year geography student,
Lancaster University

Phones

If you take a mobile phone with you then try to get it changed to one where you buy top-up cards for your line rental and calls rather than having a monthly bill. That way you can buy cards when you can afford them rather than having a regular monthly commitment.

Consider getting a prepaid telephone card or one that will give you discounted national and international calls. Ask your telephone company about any schemes that they run or log on to www.telcom.co.uk

---

'Bills come at the worst possible times and you can do nothing but pay them. Take care with mobile phone bills as they can be huge unless you are very careful (as I've found to my cost) and hide your credit card as soon as you receive it. Probably my best advice would be to get a part-time job of some description, even if you're only earning £20 a week or so it makes all the difference.'

Peter Rodger, second-year biology student,
Wentworth College, University of York

Clothes

Many students feel pressure to keep up with the latest fashion. You can't afford to do this. Markets, second-hand shops and sales all offer cheaper alternatives to off-the-peg fashion items. If you can sew, then try making your own clothes.

Books

You'll be given a very long reading list when you're accepted onto your course. Don't rush out and buy all of these books in a wild fit of enthusiasm. Wait until you get to college and see which books are essential to buy and which you can get from the library. Talk to second-year students about the books you need as you can probably buy many of them for a fraction of the price from former students or second-hand book shops. Many universities also have regular book sales. Look out for details on departmental and general noticeboards. You should also get to know www.swotbooks.com the website run by academic booksellers offering a range of academic books at around 40% of book shop price. You can also use this site to sell your text books once you've finished with them.

Stationery

Buy all your stationery from students' union shops as the prices will be much cheaper than commercial stationers. However, some commercial stationers do offer student discounts, so keep your eyes peeled for notices advertising this service.

Going out

When you go out decide in advance how much money you can spend that evening and only take that amount of cash out of the cash point. Leave cash point cards, chequebooks, credit cards and other ways of accessing money at home so that you won't be tempted to do anything rash with your cash when you are out.

'If you only take out the amount of money that you want to spend each week, then you won't overspend. Also, when you go on a night out, don't take a credit or cash card with you, only the cash you want to spend.'

Jeremy Carlton, PhD biochemistry student,
Bristol University

Lifesavers

Student support

For information about receiving student loans contact the Student Loans Company. You should also contact the Student Loans Company if you have any questions or complaints about your loan.

Student Loans Company – *100 Bothwell Street, Glasgow G2 7JD.
Tel: 0800 40 50 10.* www.slc.co.uk

English and Welsh students should contact their local education authority (listed in the phone book under the name of your local council) for an assessment of the money that they are entitled to. Or there's general information, including leaflets such as *Financial Support for Higher Education Students* and *Bridging the Gap,* both available from the Department for Education and Skills on 0800 731 9133 (0800 210 280 – text phone). The website also has more information, including application forms you can download in English and Welsh, at www.dfes.gov.uk/studentsupport

You can also get copies of the guides from:

National Assembly for Wales – *Crown Building, Cathays Park, Cardiff CF10 3NQ. Tel: 029 2082 5111.*

Students living in Northern Ireland need to apply to their local Education and Library Board for an assessment of their personal entitlement to support. General information and contact details for ELBs are available from:

Department for Employment and Learning – *Adelaide House, 39–49 Adelaide Street, Belfast BT2 8FD. Tel: 028 9025 7777.* www.delni.gov.uk

Scottish students can get more information and apply for a personal assessment of the support they are entitled to from:

Student Awards Agency for Scotland – *Gyleview House, 3 Redheughs Rigg, Edinburgh EH12 9HH. Tel: 0131 476 8212.* www.student-support-saas.gov.uk

Money advice

If you are not eligible for government support, if you have exhausted all other forms of funding or if you are thinking about going to university and want advice on the support you might be entitled to, then send a large stamped addressed envelope to:

Educational Grants Advisory Service – *501–505 Kingsland Road, London E8 4AU.* Or you can phone the information line on *020 7249 6636.*

For advice on money management, debt and dealing with people you owe money to, visit your nearest Citizens Advice Bureau. Details of local branches and online advice available from:

National Association of Citizens Advice Bureaux – *Myddelton House, 115–123 Pentonville Road, London NI 9LZ. Tel: 020 7833 2181.* www.nacab.org.uk

For telephone counselling on all aspects of debt and financial management ring the **National Debtline** on 0808 808 4000 between 10am – 4pm Monday and Thursday, 10am – 7pm Tuesday and Wednesday and 10am – noon on Fridays.

Alternatively, you can call the **Consumer Credit Counselling Service** on 0800 138 1111 8am – 8pm Monday to Friday.

There's also a helpline for students run by **Credit Action** offering financial advice and budgeting tips on 0800 591 084. Information can also be accessed online at www.creditaction.com

Publications

There's general advice about the sources of money available in *Students' Money Matters* by Gwenda Thomas (Trotman, £11.99) and sources of money plus budgeting tips, debt management and a university-by-university financial league table in *The Push Guide to Money: Student Survival* by Johnny Rich (The Stationery Office Books, £7.99).

Chapter 2
Finding somewhere to live

Where are you going to live and what will it be like?
Do you get to choose who you share with or is that
down to the university? Do you want to live
close to the university or well away from
student ghetto land? These are some of
the questions you need to ask yourself
when considering where to live. A
comfortable home, where you're
happy living, will help you study
effectively and make the transition
into student life much easier. This
chapter gives tips on how to
make your decision and find
the right accommodation. It
tells you your legal position
when you rent from a
landlord or landlady and
gives you an idea of how
much it will cost to live
away from home.

How do I make the right choice?

Start by studying the table overleaf. Think carefully about the
sort of person you are and be honest with yourself. If you feel
you fall into columns with fewer stars, it doesn't mean that
you'll find it more difficult to settle into university life, it just means
you have to give more thought to, and ask more questions about, your
chosen form of accommodation.

Who can help?

Start by looking through university prospectuses, but remember that
they're there to sell the university's facilities. If the students' union
produces an alternative prospectus then this will give you a truer
picture. The range and availability of accommodation varies
dramatically around the country, so find out as much about what is
available as possible. Some universities have extensive accommodation
to offer their students while others require their students to rent houses
in the area. If you didn't check out the university accommodation

Type of accommodation	Type of person					
	Confident about leaving home	Independent	Wants to meet students	Wants to mix with non-students	Finds it difficult to mix	Unsure about leaving home
Halls (catered)	*		*		*	*
Halls (self-catered)	*	*	*		*	
Student houses/flats	*	*	*			
Student villages	*	*	*			
Private accommodation in student areas	*	*	*			
Private accommodation in non-student areas	*	*		*		
Lodger with family					*	*
Lodger not as part of a family	*	*		*		
Bedsit	*	*		*		

when you went for an interview then write and ask specific questions about it.

The students' union and the accommodation office have details about university accommodation and private sector housing available in the area. Many have lists of recommended landlords, landladies, housing associations and agencies. Contact the accommodation office immediately if you have specific housing needs like a disability or dependants, or if you're offered a place through clearing. A place at a university which has no accommodation left may not be for you after all.

Should I live at home?

More students are choosing to live with their parents and save money while they study. If you choose this option then negotiate some new ground rules with your parents which give you a greater range of freedom acknowledging that you're an adult university student, while still treating your parents' house with respect. Get these straight before you start your course. Make sure you join lots of university clubs (see *Freshers' week*, Chapter 4) and stay for evening activities so you don't miss out on student life just because you're not living at university.

'I stayed at my parents' house because the course I wanted to do turned out to be at Derby University, which means I don't have any housing problems or have to move all my stuff at the end of each term and it's a lot cheaper. But I suppose I've probably missed out on the whole 'living in your own place' experience. However, I will still get to do all that when I leave home after uni.'

**Andy Bridges, third-year music technology and audio system design student,
Derby University**

Can I live in university accommodation?

This is often the preferred option as it's an easy way to get involved with university life and meet new friends. However, many universities can't offer all their first-year students this choice, so apply early to avoid disappointment. If you get a choice of university accommodation you're likely to be offered one of these types:

O a single or shared room in a hall of residence

O a room in a shared student house or flat

O a place in a student village complex.

'After I got my A level results I got a booklet with information about the different halls of residence available but to be honest I didn't actually visit any of them. I chose my hall based on the facilities available. Mine has a lot of stuff organised for the students – music, drama and sports. You socialise a lot there and it was a great way of meeting people.'

**Susanna Craig, first-year politics and parliamentary studies student,
Leeds University**

How do I pay?

You pay your hall, student house or village fees to the university. Each university has its own criteria about when fees should be paid, but if you get the option then pay your hall fees as soon as you arrive. Once you have met the biggest single expenditure you have, it is easier to see what you have left to live on. See also *What does it cost to live in different parts of the country?* on page 71 and *How do I make the pennies stretch?*, page 34.

What are halls of residence?

'Hall of residence' describes a vast spectrum of buildings. You could end up living in a huge concrete tower block or in an old building overlooking a courtyard. Most, however, are purpose-built with single study bedrooms, although some have twin beds so you might end up sharing a room. This may sound frightening but some people find it works well and it will certainly reduce your rent.

'Sharing a room is decidedly not for the ham-handed. My roommate had a very beautiful suede jacket, which came to grief one night when in my clumsiness I tipped a wax candle down it. Nearly the end of a beautiful friendship.'

Cherry Canovan, graduate student,
Durham University

A single study bedroom in a hall of residence is pretty much the same everywhere. You'll have a bed, a desk, a chair, some shelves and somewhere to store your clothes. There are obviously variations and additions to this theme, such as a sink and more floor space, but those are the basics you can expect. Increasingly, you can also expect telephone and internet access in your room.

Some universities also offer you a choice of a single-sex or a mixed hall. Single-sex halls are usually for women only. There may be a time limit by which all guests have to be out but, other than that, they'll be run in the same way as other halls of residence. Most mixed halls will also be segregated to some extent. This is normally done by placing women on one corridor and men on another, although usually you all live on the same floor.

Halls offer full board (where all your meals are provided), part board (where some of your meals are provided) or self-catering accommodation.

How are halls run?

Halls are run by a warden who usually lives in and is responsible for the administration. Your warden is the first point of contact in an emergency or if you have any questions or complaints. Some larger halls may have committees of student representatives who help decide on the plans for any development work, decoration, policy and budgets. These students are usually called hall reps.

However, your warden or hall rep is unlikely to be the first official person you meet. This will probably be your cleaner, usually at a very unsociable hour the morning after you have celebrated your arrival.

Cleaners have keys to your room and need to hoover and clean thoroughly at least once a week. It's a good idea to co-operate fully with your cleaner as he or she can become a very important ally. If you don't want to be disturbed first thing in the morning then find out what code operates in your hall. It may involve leaving a note on your door or leaving your bin outside.

There'll be hall rules enforced by the warden. These are designed to make sure particularly antisocial behaviour, such as constant noise, isn't allowed to run riot. For example, you'll usually have to get permission to hold a party and make arrangements for a friend to stay. The rules governing behaviour that doesn't affect other residents aren't usually as rigorously enforced, although some institutions do still have tales of boyfriends and girlfriends having to flee across the grounds via the nearest window. Make sure you know what the rules are – it can save a lot of unnecessary arguments between you and your warden.

'I was in halls last year and it was much better than I expected it to be. I had envisioned horrible people and having to share dirty public loos but in fact it was really good – there are even some rooms with an en suite! It's good to be on campus as you don't need to get up early because everything is right there. But you have more rules in halls and there are more distractions because the entertainment is also right there.'

Phil Marsh, second-year engineering student, Warwick University

---

What's it like to live in a hall of residence?

Living in a hall of residence is great if you enjoy meeting and mixing with people and has advantages even if you find this difficult. The obvious advantage of living in hall is that you don't need to worry about bills, cleaning, landlords, plumbing or even, in catered halls, food. Halls are usually near to the university and students' union, which makes it much easier to get involved with student activities. Most universities give priority to first-year students and some even allocate all rooms exclusively to freshers.

However, as with any type of accommodation, there are also disadvantages. You may not like the people you're living with or you may not be able to cope with the noise. Don't panic if this happens to you, particularly in the first few weeks. There's inevitably a period of adjustment while people get used to living with each other and away from home. If you're still unhappy later then ask your warden for a transfer to a different hall. You'll usually find wardens and accommodation officers are sympathetic to your problems and do their best to arrange a transfer if a room is available elsewhere.

'The halls here are really nice with a private bathroom! In the first year I was in catered halls which is a great way of meeting people but more expensive. You are on campus, which means that you don't get lost and you can get a grounding in the city. This year I am cooking for myself, which is perfect because I am more independent than before. I still get university-subsidised phone and internet as well.'

Rhian Jones, fourth-year European studies and French student, Manchester University

What facilities do halls offer?

Larger halls have their own bar and sports facilities and are completely self-contained social and living centres. This could be important if the hall is a long way from the university. On the other hand, you may not want to live with a large crowd of people and prefer to put up with a couple of gas rings and a half-mile walk to the nearest washing machine. Decide what's important to you and check which hall offers it in your university.

If you are a disabled student then talk to your university about any additional facilities you may require.

'The university accommodation provided to me was quite big for university accommodation but very expensive – around £1,450 a term. As a blind student I need an en suite bathroom which meant that the rent was 50% more expensive than a normal student room.'

Tony Leighton, theology and philosophy of religion student, Oxford University

What's the food like?

Self-catering options are cheaper but the practical problems might outweigh the savings. You may have to fight for a cooker with ten other people who all want to eat at the same time. There can also be a problem with storing food. Most hall rooms aren't designed to house a week's rations as well as you, your books and clothes. Food stored in public places has a nasty habit of vanishing, especially as term draws to a close and loan cheques dwindle. This is why so many halls of residence have a preponderance of plastic bags hanging from the windows. They're improvised larders for students who've got fed up with finding that the milk for their essential morning cup of coffee has disappeared overnight.

Shared kitchen and cooking facilities can become really disgusting after a whole corridor of students has tried to cook their evening meal at the same time. After a few weeks you may find that the person who has a massive fry-up for breakfast every morning and never washes up afterwards really gets on your nerves. Complain if one individual is responsible for turning the communal kitchen into a pigsty – you'll have the support of your fellow kitchen users. It is more difficult, however, if there are several people to blame. Talk to your warden if the kitchen is becoming a battleground.

Eating hall meals could be a better option. Breakfast and dinner may be included in your hall fees but you'll usually have to buy your own lunch. There'll be restricted meal times, which can be a pain if you take part in lots of activities or the dining area is far away from your department or hall. If you're a vegetarian it's particularly important that you make sure there's a vegetarian alternative and the choice is varied.

It might sound obvious but a healthy body is very important to a healthy mind. A significant number of students suffer from mild malnutrition so budget adequately for food and choose the catering option which best suits you. (See also *Living on your own*, Chapter 3)

What happens in the holidays?

Consider what you're going to do in the vacations. Many halls expect you to move out and clear your room a day or two after term finishes. This isn't a problem if your parents are prepared to act as chauffeurs at the end of each term or you live in halls where secure storage is available. If you have nowhere else to go in the holidays or want to stay in the area then it may be possible to arrange holiday accommodation with the university. Some universities, for instance, run schemes whereby students are given accommodation and spending money in return for office or maintenance work. If you do need to stay, make sure you ask about what provisions there are.

What happens if it all goes wrong?

Occasionally, you'll hear horror stories about new students having to sleep on gym floors or even having soup runs set up to feed them. There are times when administrative errors or building schedules having gone awry mean that there are too many students for too few rooms but these are the exception, not the rule.

It's vital that you take copies of all the paperwork you've had from the university about accommodation. If you're one of those unfortunate people who ends up with nowhere to live then take any

49

documentation you have to the accommodation office and students' union. They'll help you find suitable accommodation. Don't panic; follow the advice you're given. You'll probably be given a list of emergency accommodation in the area (see *What happens if I have nowhere to live?* on page 70) to give you enough breathing space to get something permanent sorted out.

What should I ask when renting in halls?

O How many places are available and how are they allocated?

O What variety of accommodation is offered?

O How much choice do I have?

O Can I choose to live in a single-sex or a mixed hall?

O Will I have to share a room?

O Could I stay over any of the vacation periods?

O How many students does the hall house?

O How is the hall heated?

O What are the fees?

O Do the hall fees include meals and, if so, which ones?

O What are the catering facilities like?

O What are the rooms like and what furniture do they have?

O Is there telephone and internet access?

O What social/washing/cleaning facilities are offered?

O Is there a bar?

O Is there a sports hall?

O Is there a TV room/common room?

O How many people have to share the bathroom/shower/kitchen facilities?

O How far away is the hall from public transport?

O How frequent is public transport and what's the cost?

O How far is the hall from the university/relevant department?

O Who are the other residents – first years, third years, postgraduates?

O Is there parking space?

O Could I store a bike?

O Can I leave things in my room/store things during the vacation?

How are student houses different from halls?

'When I came for interview I had a look at some of the accommodation. There is quite a lot of choice, with five different places on campus and some off campus too. We got to choose on a first-come first-served basis. I was lucky because I got my first choice of a student house. I like being on campus and have met people I would not otherwise have met because I'm not just sharing with first-years. However, you can't choose who you share with and they often have different interests, priorities, and even morals about certain situations!'

**Katie Hogan, first-year sociology student,
Essex University**

It's quite common for universities to have purpose-built self-catering houses and flats for groups of their students. They might require you to meet certain criteria but it can be an excellent way of combining independence with the security of renting from the university.

As in a hall, you'll probably live in your own room, which will have a bed, desk, cupboard and so on, and there'll also be a kitchen, bathroom and maybe a living room, shared by all the residents of the flat or house. There may or may not be a warden but, if there is one, then he or she is likely to take a lower profile than a hall warden.

The disadvantage of this form of accommodation is that – as in a hall – you won't get any choice about who you share with in the first year. This can be more of a problem in a smaller flat or house than in a larger hall of residence. If you really can't stand your flatmates then go to the accommodation office and request a transfer.

What are student villages?

Student villages are collections of houses owned by a university and leased to its students. Increasingly, universities are providing this type of accommodation. You may find that the village has been built by a developer so although it is called university accommodation you may pay your rent directly to the developer or developer's agent. The houses are shared by about seven to ten students, who all have their own room but share a communal kitchen and bathroom. They don't have live-in wardens so, if you're a confident person who wants to make many friends, this type of accommodation is a good option.

'My accommodation is unusual in that I live in a flat that is described as university accommodation but I pay rent to a different landlord and I don't live on campus. The flats are brand new but some people's weren't ready for when they arrived at the beginning of term. I didn't have a desk but some others didn't even have a bed! I know people who requested that they share a flat together but normally you don't know your flatmates beforehand. It is pot luck though as to whether you get put with nice people. I was lucky.'

Andrew Newsome, first-year maths and computer science student, Nottingham University

Many student villages were originally intended to house second- and third-year students but, because of the increase in first-year applicants, they're being offered to freshers. Details are available from the university accommodation office.

What should I ask about student flats, houses and villages?

O How are people selected to share a flat/house?

O How far away is the university/relevant department?

O How many students live in the flat/house?

O How many people share the kitchens and bathrooms?

O What's in each room?

O Can I stay over the vacation periods?

O What are the fees, when do I have to pay them and who to?

O Is there a warden?

O Who do I contact with any complaints or queries?

O Who's responsible for maintenance?

O Are the residents responsible for keeping the flat/house clean?

O Will I have to bring my own cooking things, cutlery and crockery?

○ Is there a washing machine?

○ Is there telephone and internet access?

○ How far away are the local food shops/markets?

○ How far away is the local public transport?

○ How frequently does the local transport run?

○ How much does transport cost?

○ Is there parking?

○ Could I store a bike there?

Can I rent somewhere through the university?

Many universities operate schemes whereby they rent local properties which they then sub-let to students. There are sometimes requirements you have to fulfil, such as being a second- or final-year student, before you're eligible to rent a house or a flat through the university. Some universities also rent short-lease properties. These are flats and houses which can't be leased for long periods of time because they're about to be pulled down or developed. They'll usually be very cheap but there's a real danger that you'll be evicted with very little notice.

What should I ask when renting through the university?

○ Can I choose who I share with?

○ How far away is the university/relevant department?

○ Will I deal with the university or the landlord/landlady?

○ Do I have the same rights as any other private tenant?

○ Who do I go to with complaints or queries?

○ How much notice will I be given before being evicted?

○ How do I pay my rent and when?

○ Do I have to pay a deposit? If so, how much is it and can I have a signed receipt?

○ Will I have to arrange to have the utilities connected?

○ Will the bills be in my name?

- O Who's responsible for repairs?
- O What security provisions are there?
- O What are the kitchen/bathroom facilities like?
- O How much of the furniture is staying?
- O How far away are the local food shops/markets?
- O How far away is the nearest public transport?
- O How frequently does the public transport run?
- O What is the cost of public transport?

What should I know about renting privately?

It's unlikely that you can stay in university accommodation throughout your time as a student, so sooner or later you'll have to rent outside, usually from a private landlord or landlady. Use the table at the beginning of this chapter to help you to decide what sort of private accommodation you want to rent and where you want to live. You can share a house or a flat with other students or friends, live by yourself in a bedsit or live in the same property as your landlord or landlady as a lodger. You may want to live in an area with lots of other students or prefer life outside 'student ghetto land'.

'This is the first year that I am renting and I find it really good. The landlady is lovely and I like the house. I prefer it to halls because you have more space and it feels more like a home, not just a bog-standard room. Go to the accommodation office, if you have one, because they are really helpful.'

Jeremy Carlton, PhD biochemistry student, Bristol University

Shared houses

After a while you'll become very familiar with the term 'student housing'. This is used to refer to a property in poor repair, usually one that isn't particularly tidy and is shared by more people than it was originally intended to house. Students can't afford to rent palatial mansions. It's remarkable how quickly you adjust to living in this sort of accommodation, mainly because all your friends are living in the same conditions. It can, however, be a bit of a shock for visiting parents who haven't had previous experience of student housing. Be

54

careful that you don't end up renting a house which is very substandard as you'll land yourself with a whole load of problems.

Under the law, houses (or flats) shared by many people are called Houses in Multiple Occupation (HMOs) and are subject to additional regulations. Check that any house you rent has:

○ a proper water supply and drainage

○ a fire escape and other fire precautions

○ adequate kitchens and bathrooms for the number of people sharing

○ clear staircases, corridors and passages.

If any of these aspects is missing then the council can prosecute the landlord but may also take action against the tenants. For example, propping a fire door open could lead to a fine, so don't do it. See *What should I look for?* on page 58 for more information.

Bedsits

If you'd rather live by yourself, then a bedsit is the cheapest option. You'll rent a room that may or may not have washing and cooking facilities in it and you'll share a bathroom with your fellow bedsitters. Sometimes you also share a kitchen. Be careful not to cut yourself off completely and make sure that you see friends regularly.

Lodgings

A lodger is someone who lives with their landlord or landlady. You may live with a family, someone who's struggling to pay the mortgage, or someone who rents to you cheaply in return for your babysitting services. Living with a family used to be a very common form of student accommodation but most students today find it too restrictive. However, if you're unsure about moving away from home this can be a good way to cushion the break. Find out exactly what the house rules are and what you're paying for. Depending on the lodging arrangement, your rent may be more expensive than in other forms of private sector renting but could include bills and food.

Can I apply for council housing?

Council housing is much cheaper than private houses and flats but you're unlikely to fulfil the necessary requirements and will have to put your name on a long waiting list. Council accommodation is unlikely to be given to single students and most councils require you to have lived in the borough for at least three years. However, it might be an option for mature or disabled students. Your local town hall can give you details and your students' union should know if there are local schemes whose requirements you'd fulfil.

Housing associations

Housing associations aim to provide cheap housing for specific groups of people and some do include single people in their categories. Again, you're more likely to find accommodation in this sector if you have special needs or are a mature student. Most housing associations also have long waiting lists but your students' union or university accommodation office will be able to tell you if there are any worth putting your name down for.

Will my friends make good flatmates?

'I made friends in the first year when I was in halls so I am living with them and another girl who is a friend of a friend. It's all worked out very well. There were a few problems at the beginning about washing dishes and cleaning the house and especially about milk! It kept on disappearing and people got very angry when they found they didn't have milk for their cereal in the morning! We talked it over and found a system and managed to sort it all out so there aren't any problems anymore.'

**Rhiannon Michael, second-year law and German student,
Aberystwyth University**

Most students choose to live in a shared house with a group of other students or friends. When this works well it's a great way to live, but even the best of friendships can crumble under arguments about whose turn it is to do the washing up or who used the last of the milk. A list of agreed house rules can help but it won't protect you from the pain of realising that your closest friends have some living habits that you can't share.

Think about how compatible you all are. Your best friend might have a horrible boyfriend or girlfriend or be fanatically tidy. They might be really messy in the kitchen or hopeless with money. These are all things which won't necessarily make them a bad friend but might well make them difficult to share a house with.

If you reach the end of the first year with ten people you regard as good friends and decide it would be really nice if you all moved in together, then split into two or three households. Living with people can be stressful and you shouldn't put all your eggs into one basket.

You'll need somewhere to escape to at times to give you and your co-tenants some space.

You might have to decide whether or not to move in with your boyfriend or girlfriend. You'll need to be very sure of your relationship before you take this step. It's traumatic if you have to move out of your home at any point but if it's coupled with the emotional distress of a broken relationship then it's vile. On the other hand, living with a partner in a strong relationship can help you both handle the pressures of student life and exams.

Deciding who to share with and looking for a room, flat or house to rent can seem like a daunting task but, providing you plan well and seek as much help and advice as you need, it should be very exciting and give you a great sense of freedom.

'I am sharing with friends I made in halls in my first year. It has worked out really well because we all do different courses which means that you are not seeing the same people during the day and in the evening. I'd get bored if I was sharing with all psychology students.'

Lindsey Wilson, third-year psychology student, Edinburgh University

When and where do I start looking?

Start looking for somewhere to live well before term starts. You have enough to do at the beginning of term without worrying about where you're going to live and who you're going to share with. Go to your accommodation office and ask for a list of landlords and landladies who rent to students in the area. They'll give you a list of reputable housing agencies, landlords and landladies. However, agencies may charge a fee of two weeks' rent or more if you lease a property through them, so budget for this when exploring this avenue. However, they can't charge you for supplying a list of properties.

'I found my house through a letting agency. Some friends had studied here and told me how to contact them. The agency gave us a list of about four or five houses we went round to look at them and chose one. There are four of us sharing.'

Sukanta Chowdhury, first-year MBA in finance student, Luton University

Your students' union will also have information on available properties, particularly if it has an accommodation noticeboard or student newspaper that carries advertisements. Alternatively, try the classified columns of local newspapers or use word of mouth if you already know people in the area.

Try to take over a house from another group of students as you can talk to them about the problems they've had during the year and their relationship with the property owner or agent. Ideally, you should always talk to any previous tenants. Forewarned can definitely be forearmed when it comes to dealing with property owners and building matters.

What should I look for?

Look at lots of properties before renting to see what is available but be prepared to act quickly when you spot a good one. Always go and see a property before renting it. Women should, if possible, take someone with them for security reasons. If this isn't possible let someone know where you're going and arrange to see the flat during the daytime. See also *Travelling around and staying safe*, Chapter 7.

'My last house was in a real state and very expensive. You really get the impression that at this end of the market people can get away with high prices. There's not a great difference in price for students and for young earners, whereas the difference in quality is great. Landlords and landladies can try to exploit you a bit if you are naïve, so make sure you know your legal rights as a tenant. Also always get a house with central heating – storage heaters are useless!'

Rob Lucas, third-year critical fine art practice student, Brighton University

---

Security

Look at how secure the property is. Ideally, the front door should have at least two locks on it, a Yale and a deadlock, about 30 cm apart. If there's a communal entrance then look at the locks on this as well and find out who has keys to it.

Fire escapes

Ask the owner whether there are any fire escapes. Some owners aren't good at meeting the legal requirements. Generally, in a two-bedroomed shared house the staircase should be isolated by fitted fire doors to the relevant rooms, including the kitchen, where a fire is most likely to start. In larger houses additional measures may be needed, such as fire extinguishers and outside fire escapes. All houses should also be fitted with smoke detectors and you should check that these are working. If you have any doubts about whether the house you are thinking of renting measures up then check it out. Your local housing department (listed in the phone book under the name of the council) can tell you what the minimum fire precautions should be. If the landlord or landlady has not taken these precautions into account, then ask for it to be done before you move in. Don't take any risks.

Neighbours

It might seem like a good idea to live next door to the best pub in the area but you may not think so after you've been disturbed every night at closing time. Look out for potentially noisy neighbours, residential or commercial. Under the Noise Act, making excessive noise between 11pm and 7am is liable for a warning, followed by a fixed penalty of £100 and then the removal of the equipment which is making the noise. These rules are enforced by the council and apply to you as well as your neighbours.

'My advice is to stick to the basic rules like paying the rent on time, keeping the place tidy and not having too many wild parties. It's all right to have a few parties but there is a correct time and place for that. Having loud parties until 6am every night will annoy the neighbours.'

**Katrina Woods, second-year sociology student,
Ulster University**

Heating

Most students choose flats and houses during the summer months, so remember that a nice bright, sunny day can make a big difference to the way something looks. Check what form of heating the property has, how much it costs and if it's included in your rent. High-ceilinged, big-windowed Victorian houses may look attractive but they are very expensive to heat. If you live in a terraced street or flat flanked by neighbours who aren't students, then they'll probably heat their houses well and you'll benefit.

Try to rent a property where you have control over the heating as you might just want to wear lots of extra sweaters during the winter months rather than have huge heating bills. Whatever you do, don't heat a property using electric fan heaters as these only give off very localised heat and are extremely expensive to run.

Gas appliances

In 1992 Clare Watkinson, a student at Aston University, died because of a faulty gas heater. Carbon monoxide poisoning is responsible for the deaths of 30–40 people each year. Landlords and landladies are required by law to have all gas appliances checked by a Corgi-registered gas fitter every 12 months and keep records of the inspections and any work done, but some don't. Ask to see the gas safety certificate before you move in as you can't smell the poisonous carbon monoxide that faulty appliances give out. If the gas appliances haven't been serviced for more than 12 months then ask for this to be done before you agree to move in.

There are, however, some basic warning signals you can look for, such as signs of staining, discoloration or sooting around appliances. If you feel sleepy, sick or dizzy after using a gas appliance stop using it and see your doctor. Get it checked at once. Never block air bricks or window vents as they're essential for the gas appliance to work efficiently. The **Health and Safety Executive's Gas Safety Action Line** can give you more information on freephone 0800 300 363 between 8am and 5pm Monday to Saturday.

You could also ask for a carbon monoxide detector to be installed. These cost less than £40 and can be found in large DIY stores or online at www.envirotecproducts.co.uk

Gas is highly combustible. If you suspect a gas leak don't turn on any lights or light a match. Turn off the supply, open the windows and call the **BG Transco** 24-hour gas leak line on 0800 111999 immediately.

Electricity

Electrical points and appliances aren't regulated in the same way gas appliances are but can also be extremely dangerous if they aren't in a good state of repair. Have a look and check that the wiring you can see is properly encased and not frayed. Old-style plugs and sockets may indicate that the house doesn't have modern wiring, so ask. And don't overload sockets or circuits by using adapters.

Your landlord or landlady is responsible for maintaining electrical sockets and wiring and should have it tested every ten years.

Structure

Check for signs of damp and rot. Tide marks on the ceiling, walls or floor or recently decorated patches are good indicators of these problems. Excessive damp can harm your health and even slight damp can make people with asthma very ill. If you decide to rent a house with signs of damp anyway, then make sure the damp isn't so extensive that it's going to cause regular problems and that it's listed on the inventory (see *Inventories*, page 63).

Turn on all the taps to make sure they work and look closely at the loo to check it works and is not leaking. Take a look at the outside of the property. Some signs of damage aren't always visible but if there are tiles missing from the roof or water marks around the guttering then it is not likely to be the most structurally sound house.

Your landlord or landlady is responsible for maintaining the structure and plumbing of the house and ensuring it is in a suitable condition for you to live in. They are not responsible for any damage that you cause. However, some landlords have written into the tenancy agreements that tenants are responsible for all repairs. This is illegal apart from in Northern Ireland. Check the terms of your tenancy agreement carefully.

'Check the general condition of the place and try to find out how long ago it was last redecorated. If it has been regularly redecorated then that is a good indication that there has been a high turnover of tenants – and there may be a reason why people don't want to stay for long.'

Lindsey Wilson, third-year psychology student,
Edinburgh University

Furniture

See whether the house has enough furniture for all the residents and that it's in adequate condition. You need a bed, desk, chair, shelves and space to store your clothes. If the house has more furniture than you think you need then ask the owner to store it for you. Don't try to cram it all into a damp attic as this will ruin the furniture and the damage will be taken out of your deposit. If you look around a house that is still occupied, check which furniture belongs to the current occupants and which will be left behind.

Any furniture provided by landlords or landladies has to meet strict fire regulations. Most new furniture meets the criteria, but always check the labels. Be suspicious of old furniture and ask if you're unsure. For more information contact your local **Trading Standards** department (listed in the phone book under the name of the council) or ask for a copy of the **Department of Trade and Industry's** leaflet on this topic by calling 0870 1502 500.

You'll sometimes find unfurnished properties on the market. The rent will be cheaper but you'll have to make sure you and your friends have enough furniture for the whole property and that it is available for when you want to move in. It's no good relying on Aunt Gladys's sofa if she can't give it to you for six months.

The kitchen

Inspect the fridge and the cooker to check that they work. Look at the space available for preparing food and remember that all your house/flatmates might want to cook at the same time. The other thing to consider is how many power points there are in the kitchen and, again, bear in mind the number of people who might want to use the kitchen. It's really annoying having to unplug the kettle every time someone wants to iron a shirt. As with the furniture, check what equipment belongs to the house and what belongs to the occupants. Large kitchens are extremely useful in shared households.

Transport

Look carefully at what's available in the area and imagine yourself travelling back late at night alone. If possible, take a look at the house at night so you can see whether the street lighting is adequate. Ask how frequently public transport runs to and from town and university and how much it costs. You'll also need to know how late the transport runs at night. If you rely on your own car or bike then look at parking and storage facilities.

Deposits

A deposit, usually one month's rent, is paid in advance to cover the property owner against any loss or damage. So before you can move in you have to have enough money to cover the deposit and a month's rent. Because rented property isn't usually on the market for very long you might want to carry your cheque book around with you when looking at houses so you have the option of putting down a deposit as soon as you find one you like. But beware of making a snap judgement under pressure that you might regret later. Your deposit will be returned to you at the end of your contract, providing the property is in the same condition as it was when you moved in. Make sure you get a written, signed receipt for your deposit and don't lose it during the year. Cover yourself by taking several photocopies, as a month's rent is extremely useful at the end of a year of surviving on a student loan.

If your landlord or landlady refuses to give you back your deposit you should wait seven days after your contract finishes and then

must obtain an Order for Possession from the sheriff of the local court. It's a criminal offence for you to be turned out of your home without a court order or if your landlord or landlady has been using threatening tactics, violence or withholding services. If you experience any harassment then contact the police immediately. There are specific criteria which a Notice to Quit must fulfil and if you're served with one before the end of your agreed contract then get in touch with your students' association, your local district housing department or Citizens' Advice Bureau for advice.

What's the landlord responsible for?

Legally the landlord or landlady has to keep the property wind- and water-tight. He or she is also responsible for repairs to the exterior of the property and structural repairs to things like drains and gutters, sinks, baths and other sanitary installations. Any other responsibilities will be agreed between the landlord and the tenant.

Your landlord should also give you 'reasonable' notice if they want to visit the property to make an inspection and/or carry out repairs. This is usually thought to be 24 hours. If they regularly breach this it can count as harassment. It's also illegal for them to discriminate against you, for example, on racial or sexual grounds. If you feel you have suffered in this way then go to your students' association or Citizens' Advice Scotland (0131 667 0156) for advice on the procedures to follow.

'We are having a few problems at the moment because the landlord doesn't have the money to carry out the repairs. We can't use the washing machine at the moment. My advice would be to try to get an objective opinion from the previous tenants when the agency is out of earshot.'

Lindsey Wilson, third-year psychology student,
Edinburgh University

How will I be asked to pay?

The amount of rent you're charged should be a market rent. This is simply the amount of rent a tenant and landlord agree is reasonable, taking into account the property's location and condition. If you can't agree on a market rent then you can apply to the independent Rent Assessment Committee, for arbitration. There are two Rent Assessment Committees which cover different Scottish regions – your local district (listed in the phone book) can tell you which one you need to contact. You should also make sure that both you and your landlord or landlady agree on when the rent should be paid and how. If you're renting on a weekly basis the owner must supply you with a rent book.

You can be asked for a returnable deposit of up to two months' rent as a protection against any damage but it is illegal for you to be charged a premium, or 'key money', before you move in. You can be asked to pay for the furniture and fittings as part of the tenancy agreement. However, you must be given an itemised list of all the pieces of furniture and the prices. Anyone charging an unreasonably high price for furniture can be prosecuted.

Anyone renting in Scotland, particularly if they aren't familiar with Scottish law, should get hold of a copy of *Assured Tenancies in Scotland – Your Rights and Responsibilities,* which is available from the Scottish Executive Development Department on 0131 244 5528. You should also contact the student advice centre at your university for specific advice on renting local properties.

What does the law say about renting in Northern Ireland?

Tenancies in Northern Ireland are governed by the Rent (NI) Order 1978 and generally fall into two categories – controlled tenancies and uncontrolled tenancies.

Uncontrolled tenancies

Generally, when taking out an uncontrolled tenancy you have fewer legal rights and protections from unscrupulous landlords and landladies. Always check the terms of your rental agreement with the Housing Officer at your students' union before signing on the dotted line.

Controlled tenancies

Controlled tenancies can either be restricted or regulated. **Restricted tenancies** tend to apply to properties that are in extremely poor condition and may have an outside loo. The rent for these properties is set at no more than £1 per week.

Regulated tenancies apply to properties in better condition that have been registered with the Department of Social Development. You can check if a property is registered by calling the Rent Registration Branch on 028 9054 0540. Higher rents are charged for regulated properties, but the amount is controlled by the Department of Social Development.

What are my rights?

As a tenant you have the right to:

O A rent book – which should include the name and address of the landlord and agent (if applicable), the rent payable (and rates if applicable) and when it is due, and details of any other payments and what they relate to.

O Freedom from harassment and illegal eviction – which could include things like cutting off gas and water supplies, changing the locks or violent or threatening behaviour. Seek advice immediately and report any such actions to the Environmental Health department of your local council (listed in the phone book).

O Notice to quit – all tenants have the right to four weeks' notice.

O Due process of law – the landlord has the right to recover his property through the courts if he terminates your tenancy and you refuse to move out.

'I went through the university student services to find my house. You tell them how many of you want to share and they issue you with a list of houses and flats that have the right number of rooms. Our landlady is really lovely and we haven't had any problems. We contact her when we need something. For example, we didn't have a washing machine and she installed one for us – we have been very lucky.'

Katrina Woods, second-year sociology student, Ulster University

Repairs

In Northern Ireland it is not the automatic responsibility of the owner to carry out repairs, so check the terms of your agreement carefully.

Deposits

Usually these are returnable deposits against breakages or rent arrears but they can be non-returnable under certain circumstances, so check the terms. Deposits may also be required for electricity and telephone costs. However, 'key money' and letting fees cannot be charged to an incoming tenant – they are illegal.

For further information and advice see your students' union. There are also leaflets on renting privately, a *Student Housing Guide* and a very detailed *Tenants' Handbook* available from the **Housing Executive**

69

Northern Ireland at www.nihe.gov.uk or from the Housing Executive district offices (listed in the phone book).

What questions should I ask when renting privately?

O Will it be a joint tenancy agreement and how long will it be for?

O Will the landlord or the tenants choose co-tenants?

O How will I have to pay the rent?

O Will I need to pay rent in the vacations?

O How much is the deposit and can I have a signed receipt?

O Can I see the Corgi gas certificate which shows that the gas appliances have been inspected in the last 12 months and details of when they were last serviced?

O Are bills included in the rent and will they be in my name?

O Will I have to arrange to have the utilities connected?

O How is the property heated and how much does it cost?

O What condition is the plumbing and wiring in?

O Have there been any major structural repairs in the last 12 months?

O What security provisions are there?

O What is the surrounding area like?

O How far away are the shops/transport/supermarket, etc?

O How frequently and how late does public transport run?

O When can I move in?

What happens if I have nowhere to live?

There may be times when you find yourself without anywhere to live, or you may want to arrange short-term accommodation over the holiday period. Your accommodation office or students' union can supply you with a list of bed and breakfasts and hostels in the area. Hostels can be useful if you find yourself without a roof over your head – some offer short-term lodging of up to 28 days, which should give you plenty of time to sort out some permanent housing. Always ring before turning up because different hostels have different requirements. You don't want to trek across town only to find that the hostel you have selected is single-sex and you've got the wrong set of chromosomes!

Bed and breakfasts won't ask you to fulfil special criteria but will place limits on how long you can stay. They can also be very expensive, particularly if you have to eat out. Both bed and breakfasts and hostels should only ever be used as emergency accommodation. Don't try to live by moving from one place to another as this will seriously disrupt your study.

A small minority of students, mainly in London, have turned to squatting. It is, at present, not illegal except in Scotland, but the law needs watching. Breaking and entering is against the law wherever you are, but provided you aren't caught entering the property and change the locks once you're in, you can stay there until evicted by the bailiffs. Before this happens, you're served with a summons to appear at a court hearing where the judge will grant the owner a Court Order of Possession. Once this has been granted, the bailiffs are given a warrant which they will then use to evict the squatters. Before you consider squatting, read the *Squatters' Handbook* £1.00 plus 57p postage from Squatters Advisory Service on 020 7359 8814 between 2pm and 6pm Monday to Friday.

The quality of housing used by squatters is often extremely poor and there's very little security unless you make sure someone is in the house all the time. Squatting should definitely not be relied on as a housing option. Remember, you have no security against eviction and could find yourself homeless with very little notice.

What does it cost to live in different parts of the country?

Your rent will be the largest chunk of expenditure so you need to budget carefully (see *How do I make the pennies stretch?*, page 34). Having nowhere to live, or getting evicted for non-payment, is extremely traumatic and not conducive to your studies, health or welfare. Rents around the country vary enormously. Most people are aware that living in London is extremely expensive but other parts of the country, particularly in the south east, can be dear too. You might want to consider this carefully before making decisions about where you want to study. But don't forget to weigh up the cost of your weekly rent with the cost of travelling home. If you choose to study somewhere far way then making a trip home, especially at short notice, can cost an arm and a leg.

To compare the costs of university campus, off-campus and private accommodation for universities round the country check out www.bunk.com

Lifesavers

Your students' union, university accommodation office and local independent housing advice centres are the best places to go to with contract or landlord problems. Ask your library or local Citizens' Advice Bureau (CAB) for details of housing advice centres.

Your local CAB can also advise on contracts, your rights and any problems you have with landlords or landladies. You can get advice online or details of your nearest local CAB branch from:

National Association of Citizens' Advice Bureaux – *Myddelton House, 115–123 Pentonville Road, London NI 9LZ. Tel: 020 7833 2181.* www.nacab.org.uk

Shelter gives advice to those needing housing and will put you in contact with local housing organisations. Call the emergency housing helpline on freephone 0808 800 4444 or contact the Shelter office closest to you.

Shelter – *88 Old Street, London ECIV 9HU. Tel: 020 7505 2000.* www.shelter.org.uk

Shelter (Cymru) Wales – *25 Walter Road, Swansea SAI 5NN. Tel: 01792 469400.*

Shelter Northern Ireland – *1–5 Coyles Place, Belfast BT7 1EL. Tel: 028 9024 7752.*

Shelter Scotland – *Fourth Floor, Scotibank House, 6 South Charlotte Street, Edinburgh EH2 4AW. Tel: 0131 473 7170.*

Chapter 3
Living on your own

How are you going to tackle your washing and cooking? What happens if a fuse blows or the sink gets blocked? And what on earth are you going to take with you and what should you leave behind? Learning to live away from home and getting to grips with things domestic can take some time. You may make some mistakes along the way but you're also likely to have a lot of fun as you discover a new sense of freedom. This chapter provides pointers on how to avoid the most common pitfalls.

'The most difficult thing was learning to organise myself. You have to motivate yourself at university, which is sometimes difficult with all the distractions available. Also, you have to learn to look after yourself in simple ways, such as cooking, cleaning and washing – all the things you never had to do at home!'

William Wilson, fourth-year management student,
Aston University

What should I take with me?

'I decided what I was going to take to university in a last-minute, really stressed frenzy and would not recommend that approach to anyone else! The only thing I know I did right was asking what kitchen stuff I really needed; some halls are fully supplied with all kitchen stuff and others you need to take your own things. Also, I didn't go to university with a mind to looking cool and I took all my home comforts with me, like cuddly toys, CDs, photos and all the other stuff I have that makes me feel at home. The only thing that I really forgot was some form of medical kit. Everyone gets ill in the first couple of months at university and the last thing you want to have to do is to go to the shops for paracetamol when you are suffering from freshers' flu.'

**Elizabeth Hardaker, fourth-year biology masters student,
University of Bath**

What you take to university depends on where you'll be living. For example, if you're moving to a hall of residence you need far fewer domestic items than if you're renting a bedsit. If you're living in rented or self-catering accommodation then compare what is already provided with what is suggested in the checklists. You don't want to end up hardly able to open your door because you have tried to move the contents of your parents' house into your room. On the other hand, you don't want to have to return home after a couple of days because you have forgotten to pack a spare pair of shoes. Don't do all your packing the night before you leave. Start at least two days beforehand so you have plenty of time to think about what to take.

Wherever you live you need:

O all correspondence you have ever received from the university, including course and reading lists, accommodation information and the letter of acceptance

O your National Insurance number and any tax forms you have

O your passport and birth certificate

O several passport-sized photographs

O any medical certificates you have been asked to bring and/or your doctor's details

O your bank details

O an address book and phone cards

O a kettle and some mugs with a jar of coffee and a carton of longlife milk to get you started

O a corkscrew and bottle opener

O a tin opener

O a torch

O an alarm clock

O a toilet roll

O any medicines you need and general medicines such as painkillers and plasters

O toiletries

O your mobile phone

O your computer if you are taking one

O lots of file paper and some files

O a dictionary and any general reference books

O pens, scissors, paper clips, a hole punch, Tipp-Ex, rubber, etc.

O towels (large and small)

O coat hangers

O bedding – this may be provided but you may prefer to take your own and take extra blankets

O clothes, shoes and underwear.

'The way I worked out the basic things I needed was thinking about what I did on a typical day, for example, what do I have in the morning? – toiletries, breakfast, etc. But I didn't anticipate quite how cold Edinburgh would be, so I didn't bring as many jumpers as I should have. When you are studying far from home, I think it's better to bring too much stuff because you can't pop home if you forget something. You can take home what you don't need during the holidays.'

Samantha Northey, third-year Chinese student, Edinburgh University

The student dress code is whatever you want. You can spend your entire time at university in jeans and shapeless jumpers if you choose to, though a smart outfit for job interviews might be useful. You will, however, need to take lots of outdoor clothing as you'll be spending more time waiting at bus stops and train stations and can't ring for a parental taxi any more!

If you have room for anything else then think about taking:

○ something to play music on. (Consider carefully whether you want to risk taking your expensive, precious music system and prized CD collection. It's better to take a portable player and selection of CDs or tapes.)

○ plants

○ posters and Blu-Tak

○ photos

○ ornaments

○ games (Trivial Pursuit, etc.)

○ a TV (for which you'll need a licence)

○ sports equipment

○ reading lamps (some halls don't provide them).

Even if you're living in a hall where meals are provided take these basic cooking utensils as there'll be occasions when you miss meal times or don't feel like eating hall meals:

○ two plates

○ bowls

○ knives, forks and spoons

○ a medium-sized saucepan

○ a wooden spoon

○ a sharp knife

○ a toaster.

If you're living in a self-catering hall, house or flat then you need these items in addition to those listed above:

○ a large saucepan

○ a frying pan

○ a colander

○ a spatula

○ a cheese grater

○ a measuring jug

O more cutlery

O more crockery

O an oven-proof dish

O recipe books

O more bedding, including lots of blankets or a duvet

O cleaning stuff for kitchens, bathrooms, floors, etc.

O light bulbs

O a heater

O some basic DIY tools such as a hammer, screwdrivers (small and large), an adjustable spanner, pliers, nails and screws.

Should I insure my belongings?

This is probably a good idea even though money is tight (see *How do I make the pennies stretch?*, page 34) if you're taking expensive items, like a computer, mobile phone and CD player, as it will be really expensive to replace them. Why not ask a relative who always buys you presents you hate to buy you a year's insurance instead?

If you decide to take out insurance then **Endsleigh** is the student insurance specialist. If there's not a branch at your university, ring the headquarters on 01242 866866 or visit www.endsleigh.co.uk. They can arrange for you to pay in instalments so you don't have to have all the money up front.

How do I set up home?

Assuming you make the journey from home to university with all your belongings intact, there are various domestic things you need to sort out, particularly if your new home is rented in the private sector. There'll be lots to do but don't panic. Acknowledge that you're not able to sort everything out at once and just take one step at a time. Work your way through these questions. See also *Finding somewhere to live*, Chapter 2.

'There are problems with living in a house for the first time – knowing how to find an electrician when a light breaks and if the drain blocks and your house gets full of sewage!'

Jennifer Hogan, fourth-year natural sciences student, Clare College, Cambridge University

---

How do I get the utilities connected and pay for them?

Get the gas and electricity companies to read the meters on the day that you move in. If you don't you could find yourself landed with someone else's debts. Utility companies will pursue debts against the property regardless of who's responsible, so if there are any outstanding debts inform the landlord or landlady, or agency, immediately.

All utility companies offer different methods of payment but tend to encourage direct debit, where the money is taken out of your bank account (usually in monthly instalments). The company estimates the amount they need to deduct, based on previous usage. They're obliged by law to tell you what these amounts are in writing before the money is taken out of your account. If you pay by direct debit then get your meters read regularly to check your usage is being charged accurately.

'I set up direct debit for my bills, which is worth doing as it works out cheaper in the long run than paying by cheque since it makes it simpler for the companies.'

Amanda Warburton, microbiology with medical bioscience graduate, Kent University

However, if this causes problems in a shared flat then consider setting up an account in the name and address of your house into which everyone contributes. Discuss and agree on how you're going to pay for utilities before you all move in.

If you fail to pay your utility bills then the supply will be cut off and you'll be charged for having it reconnected. Once you're identified as a bad payer then the payment options open to you may be limited (see also *How do I make the pennies stretch?*, page 34).

Don't panic if you get an unexpectedly high bill. Companies do make mistakes and they can often be sorted out over the phone. If you're not satisfied with the treatment you receive then contact the relevant complaints organisation listed in *Lifesavers*.

There are a number of companies that supply utilities, particularly in urban areas. Shop around for the company that offers the best gas and electricity deals in your area and change the account if necessary. Log on to www.upyourstreet.co.uk or www.saveonyourbills.co.uk to see how the various suppliers compare.

'I found it very easy to get the utilities sorted out. I found out who operated in my area and rang them up. They ask you what your address is and which services you want and then sort it all out for you.'

Amanda Warburton, microbiology with medical bioscience graduate, Kent University

Electricity

There's no connection charge for electricity unless there are outstanding debts. If this is the case then talk to your landlord or landlady and get him or her to sort it out. If the bills are going to be in your name then contact the local electricity board (it's listed in the phone book) and tell them you've moved in. Do this on the first day of your contract. If you're a first-time customer, you'll either be asked for a deposit or to pay by direct debit.

You can also pay for electricity by having a meter installed. These are run by electronic keys which you take to your nearest charging point and charge up. They are good if you don't want to be bothered with bills, but a pain if your nearest recharging point is miles away or only open at certain times. Talk to your landlord if this method of payment appeals to you.

'We just divide the electricity bill up between us at the end of each month and that's it. However, we did have a problem with the gas bill when we first moved in. The previous tenants hadn't paid their bill so our first bill was big – around £100. However, we contacted our letting agents and they paid us the money back so it was quite easy to get sorted.'

Sukanta Chowdhury, first-year MBA in finance student, Luton University

Gas

The gas supply should already be connected when you move in. If it isn't then ring the gas supplier and find out if there are outstanding bills for your address. If there are then contact your landlord or landlady immediately and get him or her to sort it out.

Faulty gas appliances are extremely dangerous (see page 59). If you smell gas then put out any cigarettes or candles, don't turn on any lights because the switches can cause sparks, get out of the property and contact BG Transco on 0800 111 999, open 24 hours a day.

Water

If you get a bill for the water rates it is likely to be addressed to 'the Occupier'. This might not mean you, although you should check your contract. Pass it on to your landlord or landlady if water rates are included in your rent or pay it immediately if it's your responsibility.

Telephone

A number of companies provide phone lines. Ask your landlord or landlady which company supplies your line. Contact them on the day that you move in and ask for the bill to be changed to your name. Whichever company you use you'll have to pay a standard charge for line rental and for your calls on top of that. If there's no phone line in the accommodation then you'll have to pay to get one installed. If you haven't been a phone customer before you may have to pay a deposit. Deposits vary according to the area and your credit rating is at the discretion of the phone company.

You don't have to stick with the telephone company that already supplies the house. There may be one that offers a better deal. However, make sure you are clear about the precise costs as each phone company offers 'deals' to help reduce call costs. Make sure they'll benefit your household before you sign up for anything. As a general rule of thumb, calls are a third cheaper after 1am and four times cheaper after 6pm. You should ask if your bill can be itemised and keep a book by the phone where everyone writes down where and when they called and for how long they were on the phone. This will save arguments when you come to divide up your first three-figure phone bill.

To compare prices of phone companies in your area log onto www.phonebills.co.uk

---

'We write all our calls down on a pad of paper next to the phone and our BT bill is itemised so we pay for the calls we each make. The tax and the line rental we just divide equally between us.'

Lindsey Wilson, third-year psychology student,
Edinburgh University

TV and video rentals

Many companies offer students special offers, especially at the beginning of the academic year. Shop around to get the best deal, but stick to well-known companies. You may be asked for a deposit or to pay by direct debit and your name will definitely be given to the

TV licensing authority. To get a TV licence, go to the Post Office and pick up the relevant form. If you're going to rent a television and/or a video then do this at the beginning of the year as short-term rentals are more expensive.

Laundry

Sooner or later you have to wash your clothes. The cheapest place will be in your students' union or hall of residence launderette. Separate your clothes into whites, coloureds and delicates (woollens and synthetics). You can wash both whites and coloureds on a warm or medium wash, but delicates need a cool wash. If you have any doubts look at the washing instructions on the label and match them to the machine's programmes. You might prefer not to trust precious items to the machine but to wash them by hand, which is also a cheaper option.

'I suppose doing my own laundry for the first time was a bit daunting and the dryers at the laundrette don't work properly so I have damp clothes hanging up in my room!'

Allan Jones, third-year geography student,
Lancaster University

Different people have different attitudes to ironing. Some people have a positive aversion to it while others are quite fanatical about ironing everything, down to their socks and sheets. If you're an ironing person then avoid all ironing disasters by making sure you follow the codes on the labels. Find the picture of the iron and see how many dots it has on it. One dot means you need a cool iron, two a medium and three a hot one.

What happens if something breaks?

Some basic DIY skills save time and money and beginners' guides are available from book shops and DIY stores. However, anything major is usually the responsibility of the landlord or landlady, so contact him or her immediately if the bathroom floods or the tiles start flying off the roof.

Wiring a plug

Most people will have their own memory joggers to help them remember what goes where. A very simple one is to realise that the BLue wire goes into the Bottom Left connection, the BRown wire goes into the Bottom Right connection and the yellow and green one into what is left, the top centre connection. When you connect the wires, tightly fasten the screws onto the exposed section of wire so that when you pull the wires they don't move. Make sure that the gripper at the base of the plug is fastened across the outer cable and not the wires.

Read the label attached to the appliance carefully and make sure that your plug matches the fuse requirement. Most large household appliances need 13-amp fuses, as do things like kettles, fan heaters, toasters and vacuum cleaners. Appliances like hairdryers, hi-fi systems and desk lamps operate at much lower wattage and take 3-amp fuses.

Changing a fuse

If you've changed the plug and the appliance still isn't working or the lights in one part of the house refuse to come on, then you've probably got a blown fuse. Go to the main fuse box and turn off the mains switch before you touch any fuses. You'll know if you have the right switch because the whole house will be plunged into darkness, so take a torch.

Check what amp fuse you need to replace. You may find spare fuses are provided but if you need to buy one try DIY shops and places like Woolworths. Replace the blown fuse with the correct amp fuse cartridge. If changing a fuse doesn't work then call an electrician.

Blocked sinks and frozen pipes

Sinks can get blocked quite frequently, especially when several people are all trying to force the remains of their supper down them. A plunger will often release the trapped waste. Place it over the plug hole and pump quickly about ten times. Pull the plunger up again and see if the sink empties. Repeat several times and then give up.

If the plunger fails, the pipe could be frozen or may have supper remains trapped in the overflow outlet. Try heating the pipe with a hairdryer if it's frozen or taking it off and removing what you find. However, put a bucket under the U-bend before removing anything or you'll be standing ankle-deep in water before you know it. If this still doesn't work then get help.

Your landlord should really deal with pipe insulation, but if there is a cold spell coming on you can take preventative measures to stop pipes freezing by wrapping the pipes in old rags and fastening them with string. Freezing pipes can be a real problem in some parts of the country.

Find out where the stopcock, which turns the water mains off, is in case of an emergency. There may be more than one and they may affect different rooms. Practise shutting the water off before you have a major flood.

Changing a washer

If you have a leaking tap or one which shoots water at you violently every time you turn it on, then you need a new washer. Turn off the water at the stopcock and unscrew the tap. You will find a rubber circle between the tap and the mounting. Take the washer to your local hardware store or DIY shop and find one which matches it. Put the tap back together again with the new washer.

How do I eat healthily?

Food is something which sometimes gets forgotten in student life. However, your body needs food to survive and you can't fully participate in things if you lack energy because your diet is poor (see also *Health and welfare*, Chapter 6). There are numerous theories about what exactly constitutes a good diet and opinions seem to change every six months. You can't follow the latest fads on a student grant so stick to the general principle that your diet needs to consist of:

O carbohydrates – bread, pasta, rice, potatoes

O protein – meat, fish, eggs, pulses

O fat

O vitamins

O fibre.

Eat 'peasant-style' and base your meal around carbohydrates and vegetables. Added protein can be supplied by a little meat, poultry or fish or, if you're vegetarian, eggs, cheese, dried beans and lentils. Fresh fruit provides extra vitamins and fibre. Eat at least two good meals a day, preferably three. Fill yourself up on bread and potatoes rather than chocolate and biscuits. Carbohydrates provide better nutrition, are cheaper and less fattening. Never, ever cut back on food as a way of saving money. It will make you ill and, if your health suffers, your social and academic life will suffer too. For ways to eat cheaply, see *Health and welfare*, Chapter 6.

'Pasta! I eat any food that is easy – so pasta and sauce, tins of beans, things like that. Chicken is also quite cheap and is easy to cook. I look for bargains – if you go to a shop just before it closes, meat is reduced so my housemates and I go then. I don't eat microwave meals generally, because I find they are not worth the money.'

Jonathan Clayton, third-year biochemistry student,
UMIST

What should I keep in the cupboard?

These are the items you should keep in your kitchen. They're also the things you should ask your parents to buy if they offer to send you off to college with a food parcel. A stock of chocolate biscuits may be comforting but it won't last long and isn't very nutritious.

- pasta
- rice
- lentils
- tins of tomatoes
- tomato purée
- kidney beans
- baked beans
- onions
- oil
- flour
- mixed herbs
- garlic
- salt and pepper
- stock cubes
- margarine/butter
- milk
- bread
- jam/marmalade
- a tin of fish (tuna, sardines) – buy fish in oil as you can cook with the oil, which not only saves money but adds flavour to food.

What should I cook?

'My main problem was that I couldn't cook and I'd never had to do my own food shopping before! My friends taught me to cook – we would try out a recipe together and did group shopping.'

Natalie King, first-year management science student,
Loughborough University

You can usually spot who has gone to university by the food they cook. Some 'stock' student recipes are given below. They can combine any variety of ingredients and all cost around £1.50 per helping.

Pasta sauce

Mastering this sauce is really easy. You can pour it over pasta on its own or with any combination of vegetables, meat or fish.

Take a tablespoon of margarine or butter and gently melt it in a large pan. Take the pan off the heat. Very gradually, add enough flour to absorb all the marg. Stir all the time so that there are no lumps. Return it to a low heat and cook for about two minutes. Take off the heat again and gradually add a pint of milk, stirring vigorously all the time so you don't get any lumps. At this point you can add cheese, herbs, garlic, tuna fish, mustard, nutmeg or anything else you fancy. Return to the heat and continue to stir while it heats gently through. (This is enough for at least two people – even for four if you mix it with lots of pasta.)

Another simpler pasta sauce can be made by frying your chosen vegetables until soft then adding a tin of tomatoes, with herbs and seasoning to taste. Or you could try gently melting a tub of cream cheese with enough milk to turn it into a sauce-like consistency and pouring that over pasta with whatever else you fancy.

Pasta bake

This is alternatively known as pasta 'à la whatever happens to be in the fridge' as, providing the ingredients are edible, you can literally add whatever you want!

Cook the pasta by following the instructions on the packet and adding two teaspoons of oil (this will stop the pasta sticking together). Fry the vegetables, tuna fish, bacon or whatever you like with salt, pepper and any other herbs or seasonings. Mix with the pasta. Put the pasta and vegetables, etc. into an oven-proof dish, pour a pint of the pasta sauce over it and put into a medium oven (gas mark 4/ 350°F/180°C) for about 15 minutes until the top goes crispy.

Alternatively, just pour a cheese sauce over plain pasta or stir a tin of soup into your fried ingredients and serve over the pasta immediately. Particularly good ingredients for this recipe are sweetcorn, tomatoes, onions, carrots, tuna fish and, if you feel like treating yourself, mushrooms and peppers. This dish stores well, so you can make a lot and eat it the next day.

Risotto

Again, this is a recipe to which you can add any variety of ingredients. A good rule of thumb when cooking rice is that you need 1½ times as much water as rice. Half a cup of rice will feed one person.

Fry your chosen vegetables, meat or fish in a large pan. When they are nearly cooked, add the rice and a tablespoon of tomato purée and fry for about two minutes. Dissolve a stock cube into the amount of water you need to cook the rice (you'll need more than one cube if you're cooking for more than one person) and add the stock to the pan. Add salt and pepper to taste. You can add kidney or other beans at this stage (dried beans are cheaper than tinned but need to be soaked first and simmered for an hour and a half before being added to the other ingredients). Bring to the boil, turn down the heat, then cover the pan and leave it to simmer for the length of time your rice packet says the rice needs to be cooked, checking it every now and again to make sure it's not boiling over or sticking. If there is any excess water left after the rice is cooked, take the lid off and boil the water away.

Soup

Soups are very nutritious, very easy to make and will feed you for three days. Choose whatever you fancy to make your soup. Seasonal root vegetables are particularly good and make very cheap soups.

Fry, steam or boil your ingredients. Add a pint and a half of water and a couple of stock cubes, salt, pepper and any herbs. Leave to simmer until it reduces in quantity and the solid ingredients soften. Put through a blender or mouli if you have one and like smooth soup. Serve with a chunk of fresh bread.

For a special occasion you can add cream to the soup and make some garlic butter for your bread. Crush a few cloves of garlic and mix them with butter; cut slices into a French stick, leaving them joined at the bottom, and spread both sides with the garlic butter. Bake in a hot oven for ten minutes.

Jacket potatoes

Jacket potatoes are the easiest meal to cook. All you have to do is put them in a hot oven (gas mark 7/425°F/250°C), check them after 45 minutes and every 10 minutes after that. You'll know they are cooked when the skins go crispy and you can easily put a fork or a skewer through the potato.

Add anything from cheese and baked beans to tuna and mayonnaise. You can make jacket potatoes special by scooping out the potato from the skins, mixing it with your ingredients, putting it back into the skins and heating the potatoes under a hot grill for a few minutes. Serve jacket potatoes with omelettes, meat, burgers or on their own.

Health warning

O Never eat anything past the 'use by' date.

O Never leave food out, particularly if it is cooked.

O Never eat anything with mould on it. It is not good enough just to cut the mouldy bits off as mould puts down long roots. Throw it away.

O Always store raw meat at the bottom of the fridge below cooked food.

O Always reheat food to 70°C (very hot) in the centre for at least two minutes.

O Always wash the work surface in between preparing different food stuffs, particularly if you're preparing meat.

O Always keep the kitchen clean.

O Always contact the local council's pest control department immediately if you spot any pests.

There are a few student cookbooks on the market so if you are looking for a last-minute gift suggestion for a relative why not suggest that they buy you one from this list. All give cheap, healthy, quick recipes with students in mind (and their frequent lack of cooking and storage facilities).

More Grub on Less Grant by Cas Clarke (Headline, £6.99); *The New Students' Cookbook* by Carolyn Humphries (Foulsham, £3.99); *The New Students' Veggie Cookbook* by Carolyn Humphries (Foulsham, £3.99); *The Student's Vegetarian Cookbook* by Jenny Baker (Faber and Faber, £6.99) and *The Students' Sausage, Egg and Beans Cookbook* by Jane Bamforth (Foulsham, £3.99).

Lifesavers

For independent information on anything from dealing with landlords, landladies and utility companies to managing debt and paying bills contact your local Citizens' Advice Bureau or look at their online advice. If you have any difficulty tracking your local CAB down, contact:

National Association of Citizens' Advice Bureaux – *Myddelton House, 115–123 Pentonville Road, London N1 9LZ. Tel: 020 7833 2181.* www.nacab.org.uk

For advice on how to change your electricity and/or gas company or to get a factsheet which compares prices in your area contact:

Ofgem *(Office of Gas and Electricity Markets) – 9 Millbank, London SW1P 3GE. Tel: 020 7901 7000.* www.ofgem.gov.uk

Or in Scotland:

Ofgem – *Regent's Court, 70 West Regent Street, Glasgow G2 2QZ. Tel: 0141 331 2678.*

To make a complaint about a gas or electricity company you need to contact **Energywatch**:

Gas 0845 906 0708 (0845 7581 401 minicom)

Electricity 0845 601 3131 (0845 7697 128 minicom)

www.energywatch.org.uk

Oftel regulates telecommunications companies and can help if you have a complaint about a telephone company:

Oftel *(Office of Telecommunications) – 50 Ludgate Hill, London EC4M 7JJ. Tel: 020 7634 8700.* www.oftel.gov.uk

Ofwat can provide details about the different water rates round the country and can help with complaints about water companies:

Ofwat *(Office of Water Services) – Centre City Tower, 7 Hill Street, Birmingham B5 5UA. Tel: 0121 625 1300.* www.ofwat.gov.uk

Publications

You can also find tips on setting up home, shopping and cooking in *Making the Most of Being a Student* by Judy Bastyra (Kogan Page, £8.99).

Chapter 4
Freshers' week

What will be organised for you? How will you meet other students? Will you get on instantly or will it take some time? When will you be expected to start studying again? How will you know where you're supposed to be and when? Don't panic – everyone's asking the same questions.

Freshers' week is something that should happen to sane people only once in their lifetime. You'll be hurled into a whirlwind of social and organisational activity and will probably emerge wondering when it was that you last had a decent night's sleep or a meal. It's like starting a new school or job but with the advantage that everyone's in exactly the same boat. Don't worry if this sounds daunting – most people thoroughly enjoy themselves.

'It was more a freshers' few days than a week but it was good, if a bit daunting. I don't think you should panic if your freshers' week is disappointing because it doesn't mean the rest will be bad – it's only the beginning, there is lots more to come. If I were to choose my top five nights out at uni, none of them would be from freshers' week.'

Katherine Lawrey, fourth-year Hispanic studies and history student, Birmingham University

You'll be sent detailed instructions for when you first arrive, so make sure you bring this information with you. Don't worry about not being able to find your way around, as there will be plenty of signs and people to direct you. The first thing to do is register (sign on as a student). Where you do this varies in different institutions. Some will want you to register with your students' union, some with the accommodation office, if you have been allocated a place in university accommodation, and some with the university itself.

By the end of your first few days you should have:

O registered with your students' union, your faculty and department

O registered with the health centre or a doctor

O joined the library and know how to access the IT facilities

O got all the timetables and course handbooks that you need

O made sure that you know when you need to register for the courses that you want to take

O found out about local job opportunities if you know you are going to need to work.

You'll acquire several cards along the way, including a university card – which usually also serves as your library card – and a card showing you're a member of your students' union. Bring at least four passport-sized photographs with you as each card you're issued will require one. Have ready any communication you've received from the university and your local educational authority. Take photocopies of all communications and keep them safe.

You'll spend your first days trying to get your bearings, settling into your accommodation and meeting the other new students. Don't worry if you don't get on immediately with the people you're living with as it takes time to settle in. See also *Health and welfare*, Chapter 6.

What will have been organised?

'My freshers' week was good. We have a system of an introduction week card for which you pay an initial £25 but then entry to everything is free during that week. I went to events that were organised by the university – there was a huge variety to choose from, a lot of different music to account for all tastes. You could even go and see Timmy Mallet!'

**Susanna Craig, first-year politics and parliamentary studies student,
Leeds University**

Your students' union will have organised at least one event, and more likely a series of events, to help you meet other students. You may be able to buy a card which allows you into all the activites organised by the students' union during the freshers' period. These can be good value for money if you like the sound of the events offered and you're pretty sure you're not going to lose your card during the revelry. They sometimes also provide discounts at local cinemas, shops and other outlets (you may also get these discounts with your university union card and your NUS card will certainly entitle you to discounts – see *Lifesavers*).

'It's strange because you speak to so many people and then if you see them later in the year, you don't quite know them and you don't know whether to say hello or not. I did make some good friends in the first week though.'

Katherine Lawrey, fourth-year Hispanic studies and history student, Birmingham University

---

The nature of freshers' events depends entirely upon the imagination and energy of the people running your students' union and can range from organised quiz and game shows to spontaneous pub crawls. Try to avoid events which aren't organised by the union as they may be a rip-off. Definitely join in at least one of the events organised, even if you're unsure about meeting new people. The later you leave it, the harder it will be to make friends because people will have begun to form groups. Remember that initially everybody is in the same position and will be as nervous as each other, even if some are better at hiding it.

Most students' unions organise a Freshers' Ball. These aren't usually formal affairs but all-night parties with a mixture of live music, discos and extended bar licences. It may be held towards the end of the freshers' introduction period and be open to students from other years. This is a very good way of getting to meet other students at the university.

Freshers' fairs

These are also known as Intro Fairs, or even 'Faires' in those universities with 'olde worlde' pretensions. They're where you find out about all the clubs and societies your university has to offer and where you'll be bombarded by banks and companies with 'student interests' plying you with freebies to attract your custom. The companies who take stalls at freshers' fairs can range from the Armed Forces to the local cinema and banks to magazines. Find the company that's giving away the largest plastic bag as you need it to put all the freebies in. And make sure you get all the freebies you can – that packet of instant pasta sauce may not seem that appealing at the time but you will find a use for it.

Most universities offer an impressive range of sports and extracurricular activities and there is bound to be something which interests you. You can try anything from karate to cricket or meditation to line dancing. If there isn't already a club catering for your hobby or interest, then set one up (see page 96). But be wary of overenthusiastic club members trying hard to persuade you to join their activity. You may have to pay a fee to join, so look at the complete list of stalls and have a rough idea of those you might be interested in before joining anything. The students' union may publish a handbook giving you more specific details about the club's or society's past history, successes and meeting times. Clubs and societies are great places to meet people with whom you share a common interest but, if you're asked for money, find out where it goes and what you get for it.

'I went to the freshers' fair and looked at all the societies (and took the freebies!) and then went back to the ones I was interested in – the photography society and the film society. I only joined two because I wanted to see how my workload would pan out first and how much free time I would have. Also, they ask for money there and then when you join and I didn't have enough to join more!'

Katie Hogan, first-year sociology student,
Essex University

When will I meet my tutors?

You'll be given a list of what your department has organised either when you register or through your pigeon-hole, which is where you collect all your post. Some departments are very keen on arranging social events and bombard you with invitations to meet the head of department, your personal tutor and every single lecturer you might ever possibly encounter during your time at university.

Some people find it helpful to get to know their lecturers in a social context before they meet them in a classroom. Even if this idea doesn't appeal to you, departmental parties are good places to meet other students. It's useful to be able to identify one or two faces you know are on the same course, even if you just end up comparing timetable arrangements or lecture hall locations.

'We have personal tutors and I met mine in the first week of the first year. This was brilliant because in my tutor group there were five of us and we instantly had a connection – we were all doing the same course and had the same tutor and in the first week of university that is all you need to be firm friends. Also, my personal tutor has been a great support throughout the course of my university degree and I think it was a great thing to get to know one tutor really well.'

**Elizabeth Hardaker, fourth-year biology masters student,
University of Bath**

When will I start studying?

You probably won't attend any classes until at least three days after you arrive, so you have time to sort out where you should be and when you should be there. Departmental secretaries are extremely helpful during this time. Go to them with any queries and don't be afraid to ask – they'll undoubtedly have been asked the same thing before.

When you register with your faculty and department you'll be told what introductory talks are being held, where you can find your timetable and how to select your options. You'll probably also be given a map of the department's lecture rooms and classrooms. You won't be expected to know where you're going immediately. Leave extra time to get to lectures until you find your bearings, but don't worry too much about being late because you got lost. You'll receive a sympathetic reception during the first two weeks.

You may be invited to attend a tour of the library and computer facilities. This might seem unnecessary and it isn't usually enthralling but it is very useful, particularly in universities that have large library facilities and if your school didn't. You'll be glad to know where to find the books relevant to your subject, how to use the cataloguing system and the various computer facilities available.

'We had an induction module week before the beginning of term. It was like normal lectures but more informal. The members of the department introduced themselves to us, told us their specialities, gave us information about the course, our timetables and so on. They also told us about a drinks party in a pub where we could get to know them and the students in other years. It was a really good way to be introduced.'

**Martin Petchey, second-year psychology student,
Luton University**

How do I find out about the area?

'My university has three sites so it was difficult to find my way around to start with. I still don't know all the parts to it but that's not a problem because we generally go as a group when we have to go to an area we haven't been to before.'

Vicky Spencer, third-year textile design student, Chelsea College of Art and Design

Some universities run tours of the local area, when you'll be shown the student haunts and the places to avoid. In some towns there can be friction between students and the local community, while in others the relationship is harmonious or the student population just gets absorbed into the crowds. You'll be warned by your students' union if there's an antagonistic relationship between locals and students. Read *Travelling around and staying safe*, Chapter 7 for ways to avoid trouble and tactics to keep you safer.

If you aren't offered a tour then explore for yourself with other students. If you're living in a self-catering hall or house then you'll have to do this almost as soon as you get there, as you need to learn quickly where to buy cheap food. Ask students already at the university where the best local shops are and if there are any markets where you can buy food cheaply (see also *Health and welfare*, Chapter 6).

While it can first appear daunting to familiarise yourself with a new area when you have so much else going on, it's worth doing. Everywhere has something else to offer other than just the local university campus activities and you're likely to gain a great deal from exploring your nearest town's social, cultural and culinary life. Many students find that they like the town where they go to university so much that they never leave!

It's a good idea to get a guide book to get you started and *Rough Guides* produce city guides to most areas where there are universities in England, Northern Ireland, Scotland and Wales. Look out for them in book shops or visit www.roughguides.com

'A couple of times every week a few of us would go off campus and 'explore' the local area. This generally meant finding a new pub for lunch. By time we knew where all the pubs were we could navigate the local area fairly easily.'

Andrew Stephenson, third-year business management student, Royal Holloway College, University of London

How do I get the most out of university life?

Don't risk missing out on all that university can offer you by just studying and finding a regular spot at the bar. University offers you a really valuable opportunity to try out new things and gain skills to offer to future employers. This is vital in an age when a university degree is not an automatic passport to a job of your choice. University clubs, societies and activities provide excellent opportunities to develop new skills and gain experience while having fun and making friends who share your interests. See also *Life after university*, Chapter 8.

Sports clubs

'I decided to join the badminton club. It has been really good. I've made loads of friends and had a good laugh playing the sport I enjoy and having the social aspect as well. We are in the BUSA league (the university sports league), which has meant that we meet loads of people from around the country, compete against them and make some new friends.'

Paul Blundell, first-year psychology student,
Lincoln University

Sport is very big in many universities in terms of the numbers of students who get involved and the amount of money it attracts. The clubs that students' unions run vary around the country but there will always be several sports you can choose from.

The best time to join a sports club is at your freshers' fair. All clubs will have a stand there, staffed by a member of the club whom you can talk to about meetings, training schedules and matches. If you miss joining the club of your choice at the freshers' fair, then contact it through the pigeon holes in the students' union or by email. You'll usually be able to join at any point during the year.

Most clubs cater for all levels of experience, from complete beginners to well advanced. If you want to play sport seriously at university contact the club as soon as possible as trials tend to be held in the first few weeks of term.

If your students' union doesn't provide a club for the sport you want to play then you may be able to set one up. Go to the person responsible for administering sports clubs in your union and ask them what you need to do. The rules vary but you'll usually have to collect a number of signatures from people also interested in such a club, outline how it would be run and present this to the committee which allocates budgets to sports clubs. Once you have your money you're up and running.

Societies

'My first impressions were that university was full of Oasis-listening Ché Guevara lovers. Not that there's anything wrong with that, but all the stereotypes one hears of were confirmed and my heart sank. First impressions were misleading though and I soon found a group of people whom I love through doing plays in the drama society.'

**Peter Rodger, second-year biology student,
Wentworth College, University of York**

Your students' union will also run societies, or 'socs', for students who don't have sporting inclinations where you can join anything from the Magic Roundabout club to the music soc. When you get to university you can use the societies on offer either to continue with an interest you already have or to try something completely new. Joining a society will also demonstrate to future employers that you're sociable and have a wide range of interests. Some may also equip you with specific skills you can use later, like acting or debating experience.

If your interest isn't catered for then you can set up a society. Again, you'll usually need a list of people who are also interested, details of how the society will be run and a budget which you present to a committee. Contact your students' union for details.

Entertainments

This is probably the area that most students get involved with. What's offered will depend entirely on where you're studying but 'ents' are a big part of all students' unions. Some unions have excellent reputations as gig venues where you can see up-and-coming bands cheaply. Other unions focus on getting local bands in and running regular discos. You can also see plays, cabaret, listen to classical music and take part in quiz nights in your union.

If you want to have a say in the entertainments run by your union find out whether there's an ents committee. This sets the agenda in conjunction with a sabbatical officer and/or a member of staff. It can be a very popular thing to get involved in so be quick if you're interested. There can be certain perks to being an ents officer, such as free gig passes, but you'll probably also find yourself cleaning up the mess long after most people have gone to bed! Although, as far as future employers are concerned you'll be able to demonstrate negotiation and marketing skills as well as administration and budgeting experience which will impress them.

Rag

Rag is extremely big in some unions. It incorporates all events students' unions run to raise money for charity. You may be approached at some point and asked to do anything from a three-legged pub crawl, to sitting on a bed while you're wheeled down the High Street. Medical students have a particularly strong reputation in the rag field and will go to extraordinary lengths to raise money.

Most universities will hold an annual Rag Week where the rag activities are concentrated into seven days of bizarre and wacky events – all in the name of charity. You can usually pick up a Rag Mag which lists the events during this time and there may be a Rag Ball. Other universities collect throughout the year, get most of their students involved and raise huge amounts of money. If you get involved you'll demonstrate creativity, marketing, administrative and budgeting skills.

Student community action

This is growing in universities around the country. It offers students the chance to work with people in the local community and ranges from helping in homes for the elderly or for people with learning disabilities to running youth and school projects. It's a great way of getting to know your local community better and opening your mind to life outside the closed world of university. You can also gain direct experience and valuable skills to offer to future employers. Ask your union whether it has such a scheme.

Student media

All universities have their own student newspaper or magazine. These may have a sabbatical editor or be run entirely by full-time students. Student newspapers and magazines offer an extremely good way for people with journalistic ambition to get practical experience, especially as some of them are held in high esteem by the national media. Any future employer will ask you to prove that you have already gained some experience in the media, as jobs in this field are so competitive. This applies to whatever area interests you – whether design, sub-editing, layout or writing. Your local paper may also be more willing to give you work experience opportunities if you've already worked on your student paper.

You may find you're able to get experience in other aspects of the media if your union runs a radio or television station. Student radio stations are increasing but, if there isn't one at your university, try offering your services to the local hospital radio.

What do students' unions do?

It can be very confusing when you first get to university to sort out the role of the students' union. This is because its activities are so varied. It is easier to understand if you break them down into two main functions – services and representation.

Services are all the things like bars, shops and sporting facilities, together with a wealth of sources of advice on accommodation, finance, welfare and so on. These are managed by a mixture of sabbatical officers, staff and students. Representation basically includes anything which students have expressed a need for and can range from shaping equal opportunities policies to discussing course problems with the university. In Scotland this divide is more marked in that there are two separate bodies which fulfil these functions – the union runs the services and the students' association looks after the representation side, though both are run and managed by the same body of elected officers and employed managers working together.

To complicate matters further, different unions have different names for the same things. For instance, students' unions are also known as guilds of students and students' associations, and the meetings they hold to decide policy can be called anything from union general meetings, to the very odd-sounding general body meetings. However, the basic structure is the same in all students' unions. There'll be a number of sabbatical officers (which will vary according to the size of the university) who are responsible for the general running of the union. Sabbaticals are salaried officers who were all students when they were elected, so are very much in tune with the needs of students at their university. Generally, sabbatical officers are responsible for education matters, welfare, representation, sports, societies, entertainments and the finances of the union. Some student newspapers also have sabbatical editors. The way these areas of responsibility are divided among the sabbaticals will depend largely on how many sabbatical officers your union has, but their job titles are usually quite self-explanatory so you should be able to sort out who is responsible for what.

'I have gained a wealth of experience from getting involved in my students' union, such as managing a budget and organising big events. The experience has been very rewarding and I have got to meet loads of new people. I would recommend that everyone get involved in their students' union. Students' unions exist to serve you and enhance your experience at university, so get involved and have a laugh.'

Andrew Stephenson, third-year business management student, Royal Holloway College, University of London

Sabbatical officers are supported by an executive committee of students who help them with anything from approving budgets to setting policy, running the entertainments to making up posters. The members of the executive committee all have different job titles and areas of responsibility. There's usually an executive member with responsibility for women, overseas students, mature students and part-time students. There may also be executive officers who have no specific area of responsibility and are there to help out generally. The sabbaticals and executive officers are all accountable to the students at the university.

In addition, there are staff members who provide professional experience, specialist services, advice, and business and administrative support. They run the students' union but are mindful of the policies set by the students at the university via the various committees. The idea behind this structure is that students' unions are run as closely as possible according to the wishes of the students that they are there to serve.

Some students are put off getting involved with their students' union because of popular pictures of students as militant, angry young people. In reality this is not the case. The political spectrum of students' unions reflects all shades of opinion, including a move away from recognised political parties towards an independent stance – the idea being that the needs of students should be put before any political agendas. However, if you enjoy political debate then you'll have no trouble finding a forum, usually in political societies within the union.

'I have had an extremely healthy social life and participated in loads of activities. I joined every society and political party that I could and have met some very interesting politicians that way.'

Tony Leighton, theology and philosophy of religion student, Oxford University

You can get involved with your students' union at many levels – from attending a union general meeting, where union policy is debated, to standing for election to a committee. Don't be put off if you find it difficult to follow the first meeting you attend. The regulations which govern them can be confusing for even the most seasoned union officer but it won't be long before you can sort through the jargon and understand the proceedings.

Most unions allow any student of the university to attend the general meetings – in fact they positively welcome you with open arms. Any committee positions will be well advertised in the union buildings. You'll need to get a nomination form signed and draw up a manifesto. You then attend the electoral meeting and make a short speech outlining your ideas and beliefs. After that it's up to the meeting whether you're elected to that position or not.

Getting involved with your students' union gives you the opportunity to exercise responsibility, leadership and organisational skills and to make positive changes and contributions to your university on behalf of students – all of which will impress future employers. You will also end up having a lot of fun, particularly if you're someone who enjoys identifying problems and finding ways of solving them.

'My JCR, which is what our students' union is known as, has supported me completely and assisted me a lot even when it wasn't their responsibility. There is an extremely good internal student atmosphere. I ended up getting actively involved and was elected onto the JCR as a policy advisor to the president on disability and welfare.'

Tony Leighton, theology and philosophy of religion student, Oxford University

---

The National Union of Students

If your university is a member of the National Union of Students (NUS) – and most of them are – then you'll automatically become a member. If you study in Wales, Scotland or Northern Ireland then you become a member of the UCMC, NUS Scotland or NUS Northern Ireland respectively.

All members receive a NUS card, which entitles them to discounts at cinemas, art galleries, theatres, travel agents, some clothes shops and many other outlets. You can also take advantage of the NUS's publications, advice, information and training services. There are regional branches which supply these services on a more localised basis. The NUS represents students' views to national and government organisations. It holds one conference a year where national policies are set and elections held. Your NUS regional branch will also have an annual conference to elect its officers and set local policy.

If you want to get involved with the NUS and help decide on campaigns and policies then ask your own students' union president or contact the NUS National Secretary at the address given in *Lifesavers*.

Lifesavers

The support to help you through freshers' week is provided either by your students' union or your department. Information about what the area outside the campus is like and what it offers is available from the students' union or in local libraries.

If you're interested in getting involved with student issues at a national level or to access online advice and offers, contact the NUS at:

The National Union of Students – *Nelson Mandela House, 461 Holloway Road, London N7 6LJ. Tel: 020 7272 8900. www.nus.org.uk*

UCMC/NUS Wales – *Windsor House, Windsor Lane, Cardiff CF10 3DE. Tel: 029 2037 5980. www.nus-wales.org.uk*

NUS/USI Northern Ireland – *29 Bedford Street, Belfast BT2 7EJ. Tel: 028 9024 4641. www.nistudents.com*

NUS Scotland – *29 Forth Street, Edinburgh EH1 3LE. Tel: 0131 556 6598 .*

Here are the contact numbers for the regional branches of the National Union of Students:

NUS East Anglia – *01992 589190*

NUS East Midlands – *01509 239754*

NUS London – *020 7561 0555*

NUS North East – *01642 384450*

NUS North West – *01524 35638*

NUS South East – *01483 575189*

NUS South West – *0117 973 4970*

NUS West Midlands – *0121 359 7173*

To find out the contact details of students' unions around the country log onto www.studentunion.co.uk where you will find students' unions grouped into geographical areas and then listed alphabetically.

Chapter 5
Down to work

You've done well enough to get into university but what are the differences between studying at school and university? What will you be required to do for your course? How much support can you expect from your tutors? And what happens if you find you're struggling?

'I felt daunted about work because you are left to your own devices. But it's OK to feel that way because at the same time it's exciting. At the end of the first year, when you have passed the exams, you can say "I did this."'

Samantha Northey, third-year Chinese student, Edinburgh University

One of the biggest adjustments to make when you get to university is the change in study techniques. In school you may have been a big fish in a small pond but at university you'll be a small fish in a very big pond and left largely to your own devices. There'll be no one chasing you for essays, telling you which chapters are relevant or dictating course notes to you.

'At some point during your university career you have to make a decision about what sort of degree you want. University is not only about the piece of paper you emerge with. Most people can get a 2:1 or a 2:2 without knocking themselves out and leave themselves time to do other things.'

Phil Agulnik, former University of London Union President

Studying effectively is about organising yourself. To do this you need to know everything about your course – the forms of assessment, when you'll be examined and what you're expected to achieve at certain times during the year. Once you have this basic information, it will be much easier to organise yourself each week.

What are the differences between courses?

If you're clear about what your course expects from you and how it is assessed then you can organise yourself properly and prioritise your workload. Always ask your departmental secretary or tutors if you're unclear about what is expected from you.

Traditional courses

Traditional degrees are made up of core subjects which you have to study and pass, and a few courses which you choose, usually in your second year. These degrees are usually studied as Single Honours, where you study one subject, and Joint Honours, where you study two subjects that carry equal weight when it comes to assessment and examination. Traditional courses tend to be weighted towards examination performance, though you may be given the option, or even be required, to submit an extended essay as well as, or instead of, a final exam paper. You may also do some assessed work throughout your course, which will count as a percentage of your final degree mark.

Choosing to do a long essay means that you have fewer finals papers to sit – a blessing when it comes to facing a mound of revision – and gives you the chance to study a topic in depth. However, long essays or dissertations tend to be more time-consuming than revising. Make your decision on the basis of whether you're someone who performs well in exams or whether you do better given time to work on something in detail.

Modular courses

'I find my course really interesting. It's good to do something you enjoy and something you have chosen. It's challenging and I have to be more disciplined, especially being an arts subject where you don't have many lectures. There is a lot of independent study you have to do. I especially like the opportunity I have to do an elective, which is an extra course you can do that gives you extra credits. It can be anything – I am doing journalism, which I am really enjoying.'

Susanna Craig, first-year politics and parliamentary studies student, Leeds University

Modular degrees are made up of courses which give you full units or half units on completion. You normally need to complete 120 credits each year by choosing courses which give you a minimum of 10 credits. On a modular course you're assessed throughout your time at university. Your coursework and examinations are taken into account, although certain courses and years may be given more weighting than others. Modular degree students have an advantage over traditional course students in that they have a good idea of what degree they're likely to get before they sit their final exams.

'Don't leave assessed work to the last minute the way I do! Consult with lecturers if you can because they can give useful advice about what they are looking for in the work. Use the library, which has a lot of information if you take the time to look, and the internet is also a good resource.'

Rhian Jones, fourth-year European studies and French student, Manchester University

Make sure that you know about the guidelines which govern how you choose your units, then think about which courses you'll enjoy most. Don't feel pressurised into taking a course because you think you ought to – you're more likely to do well if you enjoy the subject. However, you may have to reach a certain standard before you can take a course. It's no good selecting an option which requires you to have studied Spanish to A level if the only time you have spoken Spanish was on holiday when you were six. You may also have to take certain core units which you need to pass. If you don't like these courses, then remember that you only have to pass, and don't knock yourself out trying to get top marks.

'My tip is to stick to whole units unless there is a course you especially want to study which is only run as a half unit. There's definitely more work involved in doing two half units. Lecturers treat half units as full unit courses and expect you to do as much preparation for the classes. I had to write six assessed essays for my full unit and ten for my two half units.'

Phil Agulnik, former University of London Union President

You have to be well organised when following a modular degree as you can't be late handing in essays. Your essays have to be consistently good and your attendance at lectures, seminars and tutorials is often part of your assessment. Ask for advice from your tutors and take your time when choosing options.

Placement courses

Some courses require a short work placement or an exchange which is not directly assessed but is intended to give you an idea of how your degree can be used in the outside world. These are usually arranged at the beginning of your second year. Your tutors will give you information about firms that offer such placements or help you to arrange your own.

Sandwich courses

Sandwich courses usually involve a year's work placement in an industry connected with your degree before your final year. You can make other arrangements, however, such as working for the four summer terms or holidays. The placement is regarded as a full-time job and you may be paid a good wage. On the other hand, you may not be so lucky, and end up being used as cheap labour. Talk to your tutors about the reputation of the firm you'll be working for. Tutors can also suggest firms you can approach for your sandwich year placement. If you're a sponsored student then you'll probably do your placement with the firm that is sponsoring you. (See also *Could I be sponsored?*, page 25.)

'My course arranged a place in industry for me. I worked in Luton and I'm still in contact with the company, I'm doing a mini-project for them at the moment. Doing a sandwich course gives you the chance to see what it's like working. You realise how important a degree is, also your attitude becomes more mature. You learn a lot in your year out that you can put into practice later in your modules. The disadvantages

are that when you come back all your friends have graduated, which can be tough.'

**Phil Pearce, fifth-year business studies student,
Luton University**

Your work will be assessed while you're on placement and your employer asked for a written report on your performance. You have to do a detailed project which will be assessed as part of your final degree mark.

A sandwich year gives you valuable work experience and may help you clear your debts at the same time. However, some students who've signed up for sandwich courses can't find placements. If this happens talk to your department, which can help you to find a position or arrange for you to go straight into your final year.

Courses in Scotland

'Most degree courses are four years in Scotland. You can study for what's called an ordinary degree where you only take the first three years of the course but you get a lower qualification. In a four-year course you do more subjects in the first and second years, which gives you the opportunity to change your course. Some people may consider having an extra year a disadvantage but I think courses outside Scotland are probably more intense.'

**Lindsey Wilson, third-year psychology student,
Edinburgh University**

Courses in Scotland are structured differently from those in England, Wales and Northern Ireland and last for four years. The first year is spent studying your main subject together with one closely related to it, and a subject of your own choice which can be completely unrelated to your main subject. This year is generally regarded as making up for the difference in academic standard between English A levels and Scottish Highers. English students with particularly good A levels are sometimes exempt from this year. More usually though, they are encouraged to spend the year studying subjects which are completely unrelated to the degree they want to take.

The Scottish degree structure means you get the chance to study various subjects you're interested in before making your final decision. Scottish universities that run modular degrees allow an even greater level of flexibility.

'You start off on one course but at the end of the first year you can change courses as long as you do well in the exams. In England there is less flexibility. Here you can see what you like – it's not set in stone from the beginning. I suppose a disadvantage could be that you graduate later than your friends in other areas of the UK but that doesn't bother me.'

Samantha Northey, third-year Chinese student, Edinburgh University

Studying abroad

Increasingly, students are being offered the opportunity to spend time studying abroad and not just as a requirement of language courses. With the introduction of the European single market, many universities recognise the importance of wider European knowledge and are incorporating language or overseas study into their courses.

Your university may run schemes you can apply for and there are also European schemes such as ERASMUS and TEMPUS which help students to meet the costs of living and studying abroad. Full details will be available from your university if they participate in such schemes.

If you're taking a language degree then you'll usually be offered the choice of attending a university, teaching in a school as an assistant or doing a work placement. Speak to your department, which will help you make all the arrangements.

'I spent my year abroad in a small town in Spain. It was a brilliant opportunity to really get to know a country – not just the parts that holidaymakers see – and my best memories are of the people that I met over there and the friends that I made. My advice would be not to go for a big city, as that can be lonely, and to try to get in touch with the student who had your placement previously – they can help a lot. And don't worry if you don't enjoy your first month, that's normal. It gets easier as you settle in.'

Isabelle Brewerton, fourth-year modern and medieval languages student, Corpus Christi College, Cambridge University

How will I be taught?

Teaching in universities is far less personal than the tuition you'll have received at school. You have to rely on your own initiative to a greater extent and be prepared to collate your own information. Here are the main methods of teaching you're likely to encounter.

'At university there's no-one constantly nagging you if you don't do the work, so you need self-motivation. I've realised that the only person I could disappoint is myself. Your days are less structured and you have to organise your time yourself, whereas at school you had lesson time, then homework time.'

Jennifer Hogan, fourth-year natural sciences student, Clare College, Cambridge University

Lectures

Lectures are talks given by tutors to a large group of students (between about 50 and 100). You take your own notes and may have to sign an attendance list to prove you were there. There'll rarely be an opportunity for discussion and debate. If you're an arts student then much of your course will be covered by lectures.

Some people find it difficult to adjust to this form of teaching. Any reading you do in advance helps you feel more confident in a sea of unfamiliar faces and subjects. Your lecture subjects are posted on departmental noticeboards and/or emailed to you. Some examinations are based on what's been covered in lectures. Find out if this is the case for your course as you'll have to take comprehensive notes to help you revise.

There is an art to taking notes and everybody develops his or her own style. General tips, though, are to write down key ideas rather than whole sentences, leave lots of space on the paper so that you can add things later, and use headings to give your notes some structure. It's unrealistic to think you can go through your notes in detail after each lecture and turn them into beautifully crafted pieces of English. However, 10 or 15 minutes filling in the blanks immediately after the lecture when the information is still fresh in your mind can make a big difference.

'My university starts evening lectures for its mature students at 6pm, which seems ludicrous. This is the year 2001 – how many people now finish work at 5pm on the dot? And you really need to have eaten something before you get there if you are going to be working till 8pm and then possibly study in the library afterwards!'

Deborah Hyde, first-year history student, Birkbeck College, University of London

Fieldwork and laboratory work

If you're studying a non-humanities subject then a large part of your course is taught through laboratory and/or fieldwork. You'll have more timetabled hours than humanities students and will spend a great deal of your time in laboratories. You have to work on your own initiative and take responsibility for your own experiments.

If fieldwork is a requirement of your course then you'll be expected to go on at least two or three major field expeditions. These usually take place during the vacations, so can affect your holiday or money-earning plans. You have to undertake a fieldwork project under your own initiative for your final degree result. Your department will usually offer several alternatives which you can sign up for, or you can arrange your own project with your tutor. Fieldwork is usually carried out in pairs and you may not always get the choice of who your partner is.

'I've done a lot of fieldwork on my course, which usually involves going somewhere for the afternoon or a whole day and studying the particular topic we are covering on the course. It's extremely varied. You can elect to go abroad, but that costs extra. But wherever you go take a waterproof! And be organised. Don't just scribble your notes because it is raining and you want to rush. Lay them out properly or else you won't have a clue what you've written when you get back.'

Allan Jones, third-year geography student,
Lancaster University

Seminars

Seminars are discussions between a smaller group of students, with a tutor present to guide the proceedings. They can be extremely useful, particularly if the group is vocal and forthcoming with its ideas. They are an increasingly common way of teaching.

You may be asked to write a paper for one of your seminars and present it to the class. The content of a seminar paper is the same as that of an essay, but you'll have to present it in a different way. Stick to the same structure as you would for an essay – an introduction, discussion broken down into short points and a conclusion. But remember that your audience will be listening to you rather than reading your essay, so make your points clearly and concisely, linking them with a logical thread. Don't be daunted by speaking in front of your class – you'll all have to do it at some point. Most students find it's valuable experience.

Don't write your notes on A4 paper as these hide your face and you won't hold the attention of the class. Write notes on index cards, which are much easier to hold and refer to. If you're nervous about speaking in front of people and find that you shake, leaning on a table or a chair can help. Remember to speak slowly, taking deep breaths and, if you lose track of what you're saying, just pause and gather your thoughts. If your mind goes completely blank, then ask someone in the group where you had got to – this is also a good way of testing whether they were listening!

Tutorials

Tutorials may be individual or small-group discussions with your tutor on specific subjects related to your course. How often you're timetabled to meet with your assigned tutor varies in different institutions. Tutorials are probably the most valuable periods of teaching time you have, particularly if you get on well with your tutor. Make the most of them by doing any preparation or essays in time.

Don't be afraid to speak out. Contrary to what you might think, tutors don't know everything and you may come up with a point of view they hadn't considered before. Airing your ideas is also the best way to learn what is valid and pertinent to your course. Don't be afraid of being wrong – if you knew everything there was to know about your subject you wouldn't need to be at university would you?

'I met my lecturers by them lecturing me. But as the sizes of the classes have got smaller I am now able to say 'Hi' to most of them. However, if I had needed them much in the first year I would have had a few problems, because I was very nervous of looking stupid.'

Elizabeth Hardaker, fourth-year biology Masters student,
University of Bath

Your personal tutor is the person you should talk to if you have any problems which might have repercussions for your studies. The earlier your department knows about problems, the sooner it will be able to help you. You won't have to give any personal details – broad outlines will do – but your degree will suffer if you're being hounded for an essay when the whole world is crumbling around you. Universities are usually very accommodating providing you tell them what's wrong. If you really don't fancy talking to anyone in your department, then go to your students' union, who can act as mediators.

'We got a student guide for each course that gave us the email address for everyone teaching that course – tutors, lecturers – and departmental contacts. As for my personal tutor, I had to look up his contact details on the board at the union and arrange a meeting. It's not a bad system, but it would have been good to have had a face-to-face meeting with your personal tutor set up for you.'

Alastair Lee, first-year art and social sciences student, Dundee University

How do I study effectively?

When you get to university tutors treat you as an adult. They assume you're motivated to find out more about your subject and are interested in it. It's left largely up to you to select the material to complete your coursework. You'll be given suggested reading lists and websites but no longer told which sources you 'need' to consult. Adjusting to this way of teaching may take some time but there are things you can do to help you through.

'There's no one there to push you at university. They'll just kick you off the course rather than chase you for an essay. Having said that, they are very helpful if you go and ask them. I've found that my lecturers are always contactable and willing to help.'

Peter Rodger, second-year biology student, Wentworth College, University of York

Using your fellow students

Whether or not you're assigned a tutorial partner or group, your fellow students are a valuable study aid. Comparing notes and talking about difficulties is very beneficial. It's much easier to solve a problem if there are several brains tackling it and you'll get a broader view of your course by comparing ideas.

However, it's important to strike the right balance. Don't feel pressurised into working at an accelerated or decelerated rate just because your peers are. The sooner you identify your particular balance, the easier you'll settle into university life. Ignore those people who try to push you into extreme behaviour.

Managing your time

Time management is the key to studying effectively while not going over the top. Some universities run introductory study sessions, which incorporate a tour of the study facilities and can be extremely useful. However, the general rule of thumb is to work out three key points:

○ where you're supposed to be and when

○ which courses require you to do background reading or preparation

○ which tutors want work from you, what it is and when you have to hand it in.

Plan your weekly work schedule round this information.

Don't set yourself unrealistic work schedules – it will only depress you when you fail to keep up with them. And don't work for excessively long periods of time. How long you can concentrate for is up to you to discover, but a general guideline is to try working for 40 minutes and relaxing for 10 or 20 minutes. When you do stop, don't feel guilty and make sure you relax properly. Have a cup of coffee, read the papers or flop in front of the television for a while. No one expects you to work all the time.

Make lists of what you have to do by certain dates – it's very therapeutic to cross things off a list once you have completed them. Order these lists into 'urgent' tasks, 'necessary' tasks and those which can be left until last. If you find that your list is heavily weighted on the 'urgent' side then you're not planning your time well. Reorganise things to give yourself more realistic time schedules.

If you have particular difficulties organising your workload then try keeping a diary for a week. Write down everything you do during the day, honestly, then look back on it and see where you've wasted time, where you've used time efficiently and where you needed to relax more. You can then rearrange your schedule around this information.

Where you choose to work is very much an individual decision. Some people like working in a library environment where everything is quiet and books are easily accessible. Other people feel happier working in a more relaxed situation. Decide where you work best and go there whenever you study.

'My best advice is work in the library if you can. Trying to work in your room is a nightmare, particularly when living off campus in your second year. There are so many distractions. You'll get far more done and then can have a break and not feel guilty about it.'

Peter Rodger, second-year biology student,
Wentworth College, University of York

What study facilities will my university offer?

Find out about the facilities, such as libraries and computers, which you have access to. Some universities have extensive facilities which cater for all your needs, while others may have reciprocal arrangements with other universities or central facilities that you can join cheaply or for free. You should be told about the facilities during freshers' week but always ask your department or tutors if you're unclear. If you have any particular requirements then make sure you ask your university about the provisions they have in place and any help they can give you to obtain specialist equipment.

'I said I was dyslexic at my interview and was told about the Language and Learning Centre here. They meet you when you start so that they can help you with your specific needs because everybody's are different. Exams are quite difficult but I'm allowed a computer and get coloured sheets of paper to put on my exam sheets. Things generally take longer to do than for most people but the lecturers are lenient when they are aware of the situation. I always put a cover sheet on my essays to remind them.'

Claire Baldwin, third-year history student,
Aberystwyth University

The library

You're likely to spend quite a few days in the library so it's important to learn how to use it effectively. First suss out the classification system as it may well be different from your school and local library. Books are usually classified by subject matter, but you'll be told how the system in your university operates and how you find out about the availability of books. Also ask about fines! Some books will be for reference only so you can't take them out at all and others that are much in demand may be offered on a short-term loans basis only, incurring hefty fines – £1 a day is not uncommon. On your student loan you don't want hidden extra costs like that.

'One of the lessons new students need to learn really quickly is that it's essential to go and get any references given during a lecture or tutorial immediately. If you don't go to the library for a couple of days then everyone else on the course has been there before and you can't do your assignment.'

Phil Agulnik, former University of London Union President

The photocopier is a useful piece of library equipment to get to know as it will be very much cheaper to use than those in commercial print shops. But beware of copyright law as it's illegal to copy more than a small amount from any one book. Check with your librarian before you copy anything from a book, published or not. If your department suspects you of copying from a book or from another student, you may be in danger of failing your degree.

Some large universities have a special 'past papers' department where you can look back on past examination papers for your course. The library will also house past students' dissertations and theses, which you can use as sources of information. Remember to credit the author as copyright law applies as much to other students' past work as it does to books.

Many libraries run video rental services. The rules are likely to be different from those governing books so before you borrow a video check when it has to be returned – bringing it back the following day may not be possible if you have to travel halfway across town to a video machine.

Technology labs

Handing in word-processed work will be a part of university life and you will also need access to the internet and email. You should have any databases that relate to the course you are doing explained to you at the start of that course and your lecturers and tutors will suggest relevant internet sites during your lectures and tutorials. You'll probably be issued with an email address which you can use to communicate with your tutors and stay in touch with family and friends. If your university offers IT training courses then don't miss out on any free or cheap computer and IT training while at university. One thing you can be sure of when you graduate is that you will need computer skills, and training outside is extremely expensive.

'There are special areas on campus called "green card areas" which are extra computer rooms just for people with special needs, such as dyslexia or partial sight. That way we can always have access to a computer for our work.'

Claire Baldwin, third-year history student,
Aberystwyth University

115

Language labs

Language students will also have access to language labs with audio equipment to complete language exercises; satellite TV; videos and overseas native language newspapers.

Workshops and studios

You will have access to workshops and studios if there is a creative practical element to your course. These should give you access to the specialist equipment that you require. Make sure you find out about how and when you can use these facilities – the arrangements are usually flexible but there will be security measures in place as universities want to protect their expensive equipment. Your departmental secretary will be able to tell you the rules.

How should I approach essay writing?

Every student has to submit essays – some courses require more than others, admittedly, but you won't be able to escape. You may find that your tutors have particular stylistic requirements, but here are a few tips to get you going.

'Do the reading in advance, that way even if you are writing the essay at the last minute you know what you are talking about. And don't build essays up. If you have, say, three to do in a term then do them one after the other. Don't leave them all to the end of term otherwise you go nuts with the pressure.'

Allan Jones, third-year geography student,
Lancaster University

The research is the most time-consuming part of writing an essay, so begin your reading well in advance of the deadline. You won't be able to get away with just replicating the notes you take from your tutor's presentations – as you might have been able to do at school. At university level you are expected to draw your arguments from a variety of sources and it will be even more impressive if you don't only use those which you are told about during your lectures. Use your library and the internet to gather relevant books and research. Make a note of those books and sources you refer to as you go along as it is more difficult to remember where you got a piece of information later. But never, ever use people's words or research without acknowledging them. This is plagiarism and is taken very seriously, sometimes leading to expulsion. Once you have done your research it is time to start writing.

Putting pen to paper or fingers to keyboard

'I would say that the biggest obstacle is starting – it's not half as bad as you think once you put pen to paper.'

Jennifer Hogan, fourth-year natural sciences student, Clare College, Cambridge University

Starting is often the hardest part. Read the question carefully several times – more marks are lost by students not answering the question than because of their lack of knowledge of the topic. Then type or write down your first thoughts – don't worry about constructing an argument, just make sure that you are not staring at a blank piece of paper. Once you have spent some time doing this, group your thoughts into an essay plan.

An essay plan should contain your thoughts on:

O what the introduction should say

O headings for the paragraphs that will form the main argument of your essay and what you will discuss under each

O your conclusion, in which you sum up the main points you have made and present your opinion.

You then write your essay by 'filling in the blanks' in your essay plan and adding your references and bibliography. Footnotes are generally used to give the source of the quotations and information from other sources you have used. A bibliography is a comprehensive list of books you have used to research your essay. You may find that each department has stylistic preferences for how you present this information but, however they like it, make sure you are consistent in the way you present book titles and footnotes in each essay. And don't leave any references or books out.

You then need to read your essay and reread it. A key difference between good essays and bad is often the amount of time that you leave yourself to check and edit your work. Don't hand it in the minute you finish it. Read it through carefully, editing out any rambling sentences or unnecessary waffle. And carefully check your spellings. Long-winded essays with lots of typos or spelling mistakes will detract from your work, make the argument difficult to follow and look careless and sloppy. A concise, well-presented essay will receive much better marks without you having to know more about the topic.

'Don't leave essays/seminar papers till the last minute – no matter how hideous the thought of them, they only get worse if left! Make a start on the reading ASAP and make notes as you go along. Do read and reread essays and seminars before you hand them in or present them.'

**Deborah Hyde, first-year history student,
Birkbeck College, University of London**

Deadlines

You will be given a deadline when you are handed your essay titles – and deadlines have to be met. You may have got into bad habits at school of handing work in late, but this is not generally tolerated at university. You can ask for an extension but only if you have a really good reason for not meeting your deadline which is something out of your control, such as illness or other difficulties. If this is the case then let your department know as soon as you can – the departmental secretary can tell you who you should approach. You may be required to produce proof to back up your request for an extension.

How do I pass exams?

However your course is structured, you're unlikely to escape exams altogether. The important thing to remember about any exam is that you only need to pass – anything above that is a bonus. You won't be let into university if you're not capable of passing an exam so, providing you do enough work and give yourself time to revise, there's no need to panic.

'How well you do in an exam can be divided into one quarter how good you are at the subject, one quarter how hard you work, one quarter your exam technique and one quarter luck.'

Phil Agulnik, former University of London Union President

The usual rules about keeping healthy are even more important to follow when preparing for exams (see *Living on your own*, Chapter 3 and *Health and welfare*, Chapter 6). Allow yourself time off, eat a healthy diet and get outside at least once a day. A study demonstrated a remarkable and close correlation between aerobic exercise and academic ability. The subjects' intellectual abilities were tested before and immediately after they had taken aerobic exercise and all showed marked improvement. Consider spending time in the gym, jogging or cycling as exams approach, even if you revert to being a couch potato the moment they are over.

How should I revise?

'Start revising early, it may sound like it's a bit of a geeky thing to do but it's worth it! It prevents cramming at the end which, no matter what anyone says, doesn't work!'

**Paul Blundell, first-year psychology student,
Lincoln University**

When getting down to revision here are the golden rules you should follow:

- O leave plenty of time

- O draw up a timetable which breaks your day down into chunks and build in some relaxation time

- O check with your lecturers exactly what you need to revise

- O organise your working space so that it is clear and free of clutter

- O look at past papers to see what you will be faced with – see if your library has a section or ask your department for copies

- O gather all your notes together

- O START!

For essay-based subjects find out what topics you need to cover and collate your notes, books and essays into these topics. Allow plenty of time to do this. Swap essays with others on your course as this is a great way of covering additional information relatively painlessly. Try doing some timed essays as practice. These are not only good revision aids but give you an idea of how much you can write in the time. Don't expect to reproduce everything you can in a term-time essay. Examiners know this is impossible and mark accordingly. The more practice essays you do, the easier it becomes to judge the amount you can write and the points you need to make to answer exam questions well, within the time allowed. For practical subjects make sure you have completed all your assessed projects and handed in all your coursework before you're examined.

'I've noticed that, in my course anyway, some people ask you to do work that is not worthwhile, it's better to look at past papers to know what's expected of you in exams.'

**Jennifer Hogan, fourth-year natural sciences student,
Clare College, Cambridge University**

Everyone has different techniques for learning information. As a general rule of thumb, always condense the information each time you read it, so you end up looking at less and less paper. Aim to end up with just a few facts which you commit to memory which act as triggers to all you know about that topic. Draw up a revision timetable which takes you up to your exams and then break this down into daily timetables. Try to revise in chunks of about 45 minutes and build in periods of relaxation and exercise. Most people find it easier to revise one topic at a time rather than jump around. Some people also find it helpful to revise with friends, although others find this intimidating.

Don't stay up the night before an exam. It might seem like the end of the world if you don't read up on that topic just once more, but a tired brain acts in strange ways. You can end up squeezing out the information you've absorbed. Even if you've done very little work, you're better off sitting an exam with a refreshed brain. Exams are largely assessed on your response to the question and a tired brain can't respond very effectively.

Finally, check when and where the exam is, how you are going to get there and how long it will take. If you have to travel to somewhere unfamiliar do a dummy run beforehand. Leave plenty of time to travel – the last thing you need is to add to your exam stress by worrying about whether you are going to make it on time. You can always take your notes with you and read through them once more if you arrive early.

What should I do when in the exam?

Once in the exam check what's required by reading the instructions at the top – do this at least twice. If you have to carry out a project or experiment then double check your equipment to see if it's all there and working. Make sure your mobile is switched off!

Always answer all the questions you're supposed to. It is much easier to pass an exam by attempting to answer all questions, even those you're unsure of, than by trying to score exceptional marks for the questions you're confident of and leaving others out.

Exam technique is important and there are a few simple steps you can take which might help make all the difference:

1. Read the questions through carefully, making sure you read the whole paper before you select the questions you are going to answer.

2. Work out how much time you have to spend on each question, noting how much of the final mark they carry – so if one question carries 50% of the marks make sure you spend 50% of your time on it. It is also vital that you leave some time for reading everything through at the end – this might sound like a luxury you can ill afford, but careless mistakes slip in when you are writing quickly.

3. Reread carefully the questions you have selected.

4. Think about how you are going to answer the question, make a plan and use the plan to keep you focused on the question. If you have 45 minutes to write an essay question you should spend ten minutes thinking about and planning your answers, 30 minutes writing your answer down and five minutes rereading it and correcting spelling and grammar.

5. Move on to the next question when your allocated time is up.

6. If your mind goes completely blank try leaving that question and continuing with another one – you can always come back later once your confidence has returned. Don't waste time struggling when there are other marks you could be getting from other questions.

7. If you really run out of time and there is still information you wanted to include then write it in note form at the end of your answer – you may pick up the odd mark for it.

8. Write clearly and legibly. If the examiner can't read your writing they won't be able to follow your argument or calculations and you may even have to pay to have your paper transcribed – it also won't endear you to your examiner. However, if you have any specific needs, such as dyslexia, make sure you find out what additional provisions can be put in place for you.

Examiners aren't out to fail you. They award marks for every valid point you make, rather than knocking marks off for what you leave out. So use the examination time to prove to them what you know about your subject. Your tutors will warn you if they are seriously worried that you're going to fail.

Try to avoid comparing notes with others afterwards. It rarely makes you feel better and it's now up to the examiners to judge how well you've done. Instead, try to focus on the next exam if you have one or go and do something you really enjoy doing to take your mind off things.

What happens if I do fail?

If the worst happens and you do fail a course then most departments will offer you a resit or allow you to retake a year, but some universities may throw you off the course. If there are reasons why you've failed your exams, other than not doing enough work, then let your tutors know as soon as possible. If there are medical reasons for you not doing well, then get a medical certificate from your doctor, preferably before you take the exam. Your students' union can provide further advice.

'In the first year I had some difficulties with some of my modules but I talked to my head of department, who helped me and I passed my resits. That's the only academic problem I have had.'

**William Wilson, fourth-year management student,
Aston University**

Can I appeal?

Most universities have a formal structure through which you can appeal if you feel you've been unfairly treated in any aspect of your academic teaching or assessment. Talk to your students' union and tutors about what form appeals take at your university. Collect all the information you feel is relevant.

You can also be summoned to attend an academic appeal if your tutors or examiners feel you've been cheating or you have plagiarised someone else's work. These are formal affairs and you may be entitled to legal representation. Get advice immediately from your students' union.

Can I change course?

'I changed from French and drama to Hispanic studies and politics at the end of my first year because I wasn't enjoying the course or being with the people on it. Because the transfer was within the same university this was relatively straightforward. I was lucky my university supported me as I was much happier with my second course and very glad that I changed.'

**Anna Roberts, Hispanic studies and politics graduate,
Queen Mary College, University of London**

If you decide that you really have chosen the wrong honours course then you can usually transfer quite easily, providing you make the decision not more than halfway through your second term, you want to transfer to another course within the same university, and that course isn't oversubscribed. Talk to your personal tutor if you'd like to change as you'll need his or her help and for your tutor to write a letter to your local education authority. Changing modules within modular degrees can be a simple matter of filling out a registration form so that you are entered for the correct exam at the end. Changing courses during the first year of a degree course in Scotland is also straightforward.

However, if you want to transfer to another university or make the decision to change courses late, whichever type of course you are following, it can cause real problems with your funding and tuition fees and isn't nearly so straightforward. If this happens to you talk to your personal tutor and your students' union as you'll need advice.

'Don't struggle in silence. If you are having real problems, see your tutor, talk to classmates, and relatives and friends – you never know where practical help may come from!'

**Deborah Hyde, first-year history student,
Birkbeck College, University of London**

Lifesavers

If you experience any academic difficulties speak to your course representative, your personal tutor or another lecturer with whom you get on. Or try your students' union, which can act as a mediator between you and the university.

Publications

There are loads of books out there offering advice on studying generally and for very specific subjects and courses. Here are a few general study guides to get you going.

How to Get a Good Degree by Phil Race (Open University Press, £13.99); *How to Win as a Final Year Student: essays, exams and employment* by Phil Race (Open University Press, £12.99); *Last-Minute Study Tips* by Ron Fry (Kogan Page, £7.99); *Manage Your Time* by Ron Fry (Kogan Page, £7.99); *The Student's Guide to Exam Success* by Eileen Tracy (Open University Press, £9.99).

Chapter 6
Health and welfare

How are you going to get organised enough to cook for yourself, let alone registering with a doctor? Why does the term 'freshers' flu' sound so familiar? How will you make friends? What happens if you get lonely? Or maybe you'll meet the lover of your dreams. In which case how are you going to look after your sexual health? And then there's drugs ...

'It was a bit of a culture shock starting university. On the first day when your parents leave you in your room, with all your stuff just dumped there, it takes a while to sink in. But then you meet other people and talk to them, which takes your mind off things. Everybody else is in the same situation. You can always go home at the weekends if you want to, which I did a lot to begin with. Now I'm much more independent.'

Phil Pearce, fifth-year business studies student, Luton University

It can seem very daunting to be faced with so much all at once without the support of your family at home. But, as long as you don't try to do everything at once and follow some basic rules, you should remain healthy and happy. Rule number one – don't skip meals. Your body needs regular food to be able to cope with the stresses of moving, starting your course and making new friends. Rule number two – make sure you get as much sleep as you need. Different people need varying amounts of sleep so don't feel pressurised into staying up all night if you can't function without your eight hours.

Why do so many freshers get ill?

There is a great temptation, particularly when you first get to university, to burn the candle at both ends. If you're doing this while trying to get used to living away from home for the first time then you're likely to encounter the range of maladies known as 'freshers' flu'.

'Keep your body clock in check, especially in the first year, when there is a real pressure to stay up late during the week so it can be hard to get up for lectures.'

Allan Jones, third-year geography student,
Lancaster University

Flu, colds and coughs

These usually strike when you're run down, and can rapidly do the rounds in halls of residence. There's still no magic cure, but you can do certain things to make yourself feel better. Try taking paracetamol or aspirin, tucking yourself into bed and drinking lots of fluids. See the doctor if your symptoms persist for more than three days or if you feel worse rather than better.

Sore throats

These can be very nasty and make you feel lousy. Try gargling with TCP or soluble aspirin as this may ease the pain. If you don't feel like eating much drink plenty of fluids. See your doctor if your throat doesn't get better after a couple of days, if you can't swallow or if you have earache as well.

Headaches

These are caused by a number of different things – not just hangovers – and will normally go away in a few hours if you take paracetamol or aspirin. However, if you have severe or frequent headaches then go and see your doctor. If you have a constant headache with fever or your neck feels stiff, call your doctor immediately (see *Meningitis*, page 128).

'I've had colds and flu and stuff. The best thing is to go down to the pharmacy and tell them what you have and ask them what they think is best.'

Paul Blundell, first-year psychology student,
Lincoln University

Stress and anxiety

Stress is very high among students when they first move to university because they have to deal with a lot of changes all at once. The symptoms of stress come in different forms, like feeling tired all the time or not being able to sleep at all, and you're the best person to know whether or not you're suffering. If your symptoms are extreme then you may be suffering from anxiety.

Don't be afraid of talking about your symptoms, they aren't trivial. Many, many students suffer from stress, so you're definitely not alone. Many find that exercise helps relieve the symptoms and there are various relaxation techniques that can help. Get advice from your GP, who can refer you to a therapist or prescribe medication if your symptoms are extreme.

Eating disorders

There's not much we can do about our general body shape, just as we can't change the colour of our eyes. If you eat a healthy diet (see *Living on your own*, Chapter 3) then your body will stabilise at a weight which is healthy and normal for you. The easiest way to work out if you're the correct weight for you is to work out your Body Mass Index (BMI). Take your weight in kilos and divide it by your height in metres squared. A 'normal' range is between 20 and 25. Your BMI shouldn't be below 18 and if it's over 30 then you're overweight, medically speaking. If you need to lose weight seek advice from your GP.

Many people don't realise they are suffering from an eating disorder as problems with food have a variety of underlying psychological causes. The anxieties brought on by the stress of starting at university can sometimes manifest themselves as eating disorders.

There are three main types of eating disorder: anorexia nervosa, when people consistently don't eat as much as they need; bulimia, a cycle of binge eating followed by starvation or other forms of purging such as making yourself sick, and compulsive eating. In the United States bulimia is so common among young women college students it is known as the 'college girl disease'.

Doctors are very aware of the serious effects of eating disorders and are sympathetic when approached for treatment. It's vital that you seek expert advice if you have problems with food. Eating disorders can kill people. Speak to your GP or to the Eating Disorders Association, which offers information, advice, details of support networks and publications for both women and men worried about their eating or who have eating disorders:

Eating Disorders Association – 103 Prince of Wales Road, Norwich NR1 1DW. Tel: 01603 621414. www.edauk.com

There's also online chat and resources, plus personal stories, information and advice for people with eating disorders, their families and friends at www.somethingfishy.org

Meningitis

Despite the high-profile cases that get reported in the press, meningitis is a rare disease. However, it develops quickly and can kill, so any symptoms need to be taken seriously. It can be caused by both viruses and bacteria, but the bacterial form is more dangerous. The bacteria can spread by prolonged intimate contact such as kissing, but also among people who live and work closely together. It is estimated that students are twice as vulnerable to meningitis as others in the 18–25-year-old group – particularly those who live in halls of residence.

You can gain protection from some forms of meningitis through injections and the practice nurse at the doctor's surgery can organise this for you if your immunisations aren't up to date.

The best chance for effective treatment of meningitis and recovery is if it is recognised early. Initial symptoms can be confused with other illnesses, such as flu or having a bad hangover, but someone with meningitis deteriorates more rapidly. The symptoms to look out for are:

O severe headache

O stiff neck

O dislike of bright lights

O fever and/or vomiting

O drowsiness or going in and out of consciousness

O a red 'pimply' rash that doesn't turn white when a glass is pressed against it (although only about 40% of people with meningitis develop the rash).

Bacterial meningitis can also cause septicaemia (blood poisoning). Meningitis with septicaemia is four times as deadly as meningitis without, though not as deadly as septicaemia without the meningitis. Symptoms of septicaemia include:

O the rash

O fever and vomiting, but not in all cases

O cold hands and feet

○ rapid breathing

○ pain in the joints, muscles and stomach, maybe with diarrhoea

○ drowsiness or going in and out of consciousness.

These symptoms can occur in any order and not everyone will exhibit all of them, so if there is any doubt at all call for medical assistance. If a doctor is not readily available then call 999 for an ambulance.

For more advice on meningitis see NHS Direct in the *Lifesavers* section at the end of this chapter or contact the **Meningitis Trust** at www.meningitis-trust.org.uk or ring their 24-hour helpline on 0845 6000 800.

Which doctor should I register with?

It may not seem like your most pressing task when you arrive at your new university but registering with a doctor should be done as soon as possible. Don't worry about registering with a different practice from the one you've been going to for years. You can return to your home GP in the holidays as a visitor, but this is no good if you're ill during term time. You do need to register with a doctor in your university town because this is where you'll be spending at least 33 weeks of the year.

Your university will have a doctor either on site or a practice close by which it recommends. You'll be given details in the first few days. You don't have to register with the university doctor if you don't want to but you need to register with a surgery in whose 'catchment area' you live. This way you'll be entitled to home visits should you need them. Details of doctors are found in local libraries or from the local Family Practitioners' Committee (listed in the phone book).

Wherever you register you need your medical card, even if your university has asked you to bring a medical form from your previous doctor. If you've lost your medical card go to a local surgery and fill in an application for a new one.

'I haven't been seriously ill but I have had tonsillitis and stomachaches. All I did was go to the doctor, who sorted it out. I registered with a doctor a few weeks into the first year and so there was no problem seeing one.'

Rhiannon Michael, second-year law and German student, Aberystwyth University

Remember to register with a dentist as well. You may have to try several before you find one that is not oversubscribed. Some hospitals provide emergency treatment, but this is not a method you should rely on.

Alternative therapists

If you're not happy with conventional medicine then talk to your doctor about alternatives. Many doctors have a positive attitude and are happy to discuss the options. The NHS now recognises the benefits of homoeopathic medicine, which uses natural herbs and products to treat ailments. Other practices such as acupuncture and osteopathy are also recognised as beneficial. However, there's always a danger, particularly when you're feeling ill and vulnerable, that you'll be persuaded into believing in some apparently magical cure. Stick to alternatives which already have an established reputation, talk to your doctor and use alternative remedies in conjunction with mainstream practices.

For information and a list of practising homeopathic doctors, clinics, hospitals and pharmacists, contact:

British Homeopathic Association – *15 Clerkenwell Close, London EC1R 0AA. Tel: 020 7566 7800.* www.trusthomeopathy.org

Medical charges

Full-time students under 19 are entitled to free medical treatment. This includes prescription charges and dental treatment. Students under 18 are eligible for free sight tests. Once you pass your 18th or 19th birthday you have to go through the mound of paperwork that proves you are on a low income. Tackle this early, particularly if you need medication on a regular basis, as it can take a month or longer for your claim to be assessed. Pick up the relevant form (HC1) and leaflets which explain benefits, refunds and how to claim – they are available from doctors, dentists, opticians and hospitals or you may find that your students' union has a stock. You will need to fill it out and return it to **Benefits Agency** – Health Benefits Division, Freepost, HBD.

Womens' health

Many women prefer to be seen by a female doctor. You have the right to choose, so if your practice does not have a woman registered with it then ask for a list of well women clinics or practices with registered women doctors available in the area.

Breast examinations

Examine your breasts once a month, ideally just after your last period, as this is when the breasts are smallest and any changes are more visible. Check for any nipple secretions, changes in the nipple, lumps, dimples or swelling. Your doctor, well woman clinic or family planning clinic can show you how to examine yourself correctly. If you notice any changes, don't panic as the vast majority are completely harmless, but go to your doctor as soon as you can.

Cervical smears

Cancer of the cervix can usually be cured if it's caught early enough. The tests are slightly uncomfortable but not painful. Every woman should have a smear test once every three to five years. Your doctor will send you a letter when your smear test is due. If you don't get a letter then ask for an appointment. The test only takes a few minutes and is well worth undergoing for the protection of your health.

'I had a smear test because I changed from the cap to the pill. Within a year I had gone from a completely clear test to one which showed I had pre-cancerous cells. Because this was spotted in time I was declared fit after laser treatment. It was a very worrying time but I am extremely glad I followed my doctor's advice and had regular tests. I don't even want to think about what would have happened if I hadn't.'

Graduate, School of Oriental and African Studies, University of London

Toxic Shock Syndrome (TSS)

TSS is believed to be caused by using tampons. Typical symptoms are quite similar to those of the flu virus, followed by diarrhoea, high temperature, vomiting, skin rashes on hands and feet, double vision and hair loss. These symptoms develop quickly and must be treated immediately as women can die from TSS. Tampon manufacturers recognise the potential dangers of tampon use and most include detailed instructions on how to use them safely. However, always use the correct absorbency and change them regularly. It's advisable not to use tampons overnight.

Men's health

Men should get into the habit of examining their testes every month and checking for any changes or signs of abnormalities. If you find any lumps or changes they're likely to be harmless, but get them checked out by your doctor, not least for your peace of mind.

Can I be sure of my sexuality?

There is no 'norm' to which you have to conform. Your own sexuality is up to you to define, so don't feel pressurised, either by peers or sexual partners, into doing anything you don't feel comfortable with. Learning what gives you pleasure and how to talk about this with a partner are part of developing your sexuality.

The person who claims to have a trouble-free sex life the whole time is probably lying. And people who claim to be having sex all the time are probably lying too. Don't feel you have to 'keep up with the crowd'. The number of sexual partners you have is not a sign of maturity and you don't need to have a sexual relationship to prove you're an adult. Respect for your body and emotions shows greater maturity and you'll know when it is right for you to sleep with someone.

Some people choose going to university as the time to come out since students tend to be less hostile than some people outside. If you're gay, lesbian or bisexual you'll find lots of points of support at university. Your students' union should have a gay, lesbian and bisexual club where you can meet other students who share your sexuality, take part in activities and receive any support you might need. If there's no such club at your university then ask your union about setting one up. You can also talk to and get advice, information and counselling 24-hours a day from the **Lesbian and Gay Switchboard** on 020 7837 7324.

If, however, your experience of coming out at university is not a happy one then seek support immediately. Gay men and lesbian women should not be put in a position where they are made to feel ashamed or are insulted because of their sexuality – they are as valid forms of sexuality as heterosexuality. If you're a victim of homophobia then talk to the welfare officer, the lesbian, gay and bisexual group or the lesbian and gay officer in your students' union. Don't blame yourself. Depending on the severity of your complaint, the union will speak to the harasser, ban them from the union or implement a full disciplinary hearing involving the university. Unlike the outside world where the law is often vague or silent on the rights of gay men and lesbians, students' unions have set policies to protect their homosexual students so don't be afraid to speak out.

Alternatively, you can get information and advice from the campaigning organisation **Stonewall** on 020 7881 9400 www.stonewall.org.uk

How can I stay safe and sexy?

Sex is, and should be, fun and fulfilling. However, it doesn't come without responsibilities. Most students don't want to become parents or catch a sexually transmitted disease. You both need to take responsibility for practising safer sex. Be safe, not sorry.

'The student welfare officer did a speech at the beginning of the first year telling us all we needed to know – the different types of contraception available and the facilities there are to get them. They are available through going to the doctor that you are registered with and there are condom machines in all the toilets here.'

Katrina Woods, second-year sociology student,
Ulster University

The only way to be completely safe is by not having penetrative sex. This doesn't mean that you can't explore what turns each other on. Massage, masturbation, kissing and stroking are all safe, sexy ways to explore each other's bodies. However, if you're going to have penetrative sex – and most people do while they're at university – then make sure you're both sussed about contraception.

Which form of contraception should I use?

No contraceptive method is 100% safe and some do have side effects, so take time to find the method which suits you both. Consider contraception and safer sex together. You can get contraception free from your GP practice if it has the letter C after its name. If it doesn't provide this service, your doctor can give you details of family planning clinics or well women clinics in the area.

Condoms

A condom, also known as a sheath, rubber or johnny, is a thin rubber cover placed on the erect penis. It's the best protection against STDs, including AIDS and, if used correctly, is about 95% effective in preventing unwanted pregnancy. It's even more effective if used with a spermicide pessary or jelly. If you need to, always use a water-based lubricant such as KY Jelly with condoms because oil-based lubricants like Vaseline can damage them. Condoms have no side effects on your health.

'It's amazing how many people think condoms only last for a few days. It's a condom, not a yoghurt! They last for years but should not be used after the expiry date.'

Phil Mitchel, former Welfare Officer,
Bangor University

Use condoms which have the heart-shaped British Standards kitemark, and don't use condoms past their expiry date – although an old condom is better than none. Read the instructions carefully as, unless you use them correctly, you may as well not bother.

Put a condom on when the penis is erect, before penetration. Unroll the condom with the rubber rim on the outside. Put it over the tip of the penis then unroll it to the base. Squeeze the end of the condom while you unroll it as this gives the sperm somewhere to go. Withdraw the penis immediately after ejaculation, as a condom will slip off a penis that's getting smaller. Remove the penis, holding the condom firmly at the base so no sperm can escape. Tie a knot in the condom, wrap it in tissue and throw it away, but not down the loo – loos can get blocked or, if the condom makes it out, it ends up in the sea, where it bobs around among the fish for ages before breaking down.

The female condom is similar to the male condom but fits into the vagina. It can take a bit of getting used to and probably isn't for first sexual encounters. It provides the same protection against unwanted pregnancies and STDs and has no side effects on your health.

Pessaries

These are spermicidal capsules inserted into the vagina before intercourse. They provide added protection when used with barrier methods of contraception such as condoms, caps and diaphragms. Women should use pessaries particularly during the most fertile period of their cycle.

The pill

There are two main types of contraceptive pill. The combined pill contains progesterone and oestrogen, which work together to prevent ovulation. The mini-pill contains only progesterone, which alters the cervical mucus so that the sperm can't get through, and changes the lining of the uterus so it doesn't accept the egg. Most pills are taken for 21 days and then left for seven days, during which time you'll have a period, but you should follow the instructions on the packet carefully.

The varieties of pill differ in strength and you will need to consult your doctor or family planning clinic so they can sort out which one is likely to suit you best. You must be open with them. Be prepared to experiment until you find a make which suits you.

The pill has the highest success rate in preventing pregnancy, providing you take it as prescribed. However, there are certain circumstances which reduce its effectiveness, such as an upset stomach or if you're taking antibiotics. Ask what these are when taking contraceptive advice and consult your doctor or family planning clinic if you have unprotected sex under these circumstances.

Some women are lucky and find that the pill suits them immediately. Others suffer side effects, such as bloating, depression and nausea and the pill has been linked to reduced fertility after long-term use. Some studies have associated long-term use with an increased risk of cancer, thrombosis and other potentially life-threatening diseases. The risk increases again if you're a smoker. Always take medical advice. The pill doesn't protect against STDs or HIV, so should be used with a condom.

The diaphragm or cap

This is a rubber device inserted into the vagina to cover the cervix up to three hours before sex. It needs to be left there for six hours after sex. Its effectiveness depends on how you use it and it must be used with a spermicide. Also it has to be fitted initially by your doctor or clinic and should be checked regularly with your contraceptive adviser or GP. It provides limited protection from STDs and HIV.

Intra-uterine device (IUD) or coil

This is a plastic tubing coil coated in metal that's inserted into the uterus by a doctor and prevents the egg from settling in the uterus. The coil can cause damage to the uterus, which may affect future fertility and cause heavy periods. It is not always effective and can cause serious problems if you get pregnant. It's not usually recommended for young women who haven't had children.

Sponge

A circular soft sponge impregnated with a spermicide which is inserted into the vagina before sex. It's only about 75 per cent effective.

Natural rhythm

The basic idea is that you avoid sex during a woman's most fertile time (12 to 16 days before her next period) but this is very difficult to calculate as women's menstrual cycles can alter dramatically. It involves taking your temperature every day and drawing up charts and doing complicated calculations. You also have to have a very regular cycle for this to be at all effective. The risk of pregnancy is very high.

Withdrawal

The man withdraws before ejaculation. This is also a very unreliable method of contraception as men often 'leak' before coming and each 2ml of spunk contains about 20,000,000 sperm. Don't believe the old myths about not being able to get pregnant unless a man has an orgasm.

'I haven't really needed to get much contraceptive advice because I see my doctor at home, but I know that if I do want to see someone about it there are people at uni. There is a clinic on campus in the medical centre that gives advice.'

Natalie King, first-year management science student,
Loughborough University

What happens if my contraception fails or I have unprotected sex?

Accidents can happen. If you're in this position then you can take the morning-after pill. It should only be taken in emergencies and never as a regular form of contraception. Its name is misleading as you can take it up to 72 hours after you've had sex. It is available free from doctors, family planning clinics or sexual health clinics or over the counter at chemists for about £20. It contains a large dose of the normal contraceptive pill and may make you feel ill for a few hours or even days afterwards.

Brook Advisory Centres offer free sex advice and contraception, available online or in centres round the country where you can also get pregnancy tests and relationship counselling for under 25s.

Brook Advisory Centres – *Studio 421, Highgate Studios, 51–79 Highgate Road, London NW5 1TL. Tel: 0800 0185023.*
www.brook.org.uk

Your GP can also refer you to **Family Planning Clinics** in your area for contraception advice and pregnancy testing or you can look up the details of your nearest one in the phone book (listed under 'Family Planning').

Pregnancy

Signs of pregnancy are missed periods, nausea, vomiting and breast tenderness. If you think you might be pregnant then burying your head in the sand and hoping it isn't true might be appealing but won't help you to deal with the consequences. You can buy pregnancy-testing kits from the chemist which are very simple and accurate. If you get a positive result then see your GP to get it confirmed and discuss the options.

If you choose to have an abortion the earlier it's done, the safer the operation. You can have an abortion through the NHS or a private clinic. The NHS treatment is free but you may have to wait for up to eight weeks. Private treatment is quicker but you'll have to pay. The date of pregnancy is calculated from the first day of your last period unless you're particularly irregular, but an examination by your doctor will give you a rough estimate. Abortions are usually carried out between seven and 12 weeks from your last period. If you suffer depression following your abortion seek expert advice from your GP.

You can get information and advice on your options when facing an unwanted pregnancy, including counselling and abortions offered in centres round the country in collaboration with the NHS from:

British Pregnancy Advisory Service – *Austy Manor, Wootton Wawen, Solihull, West Midlands B95 6BX. Tel: 08457 304030.*
www.bpas.org.uk

If you choose to continue with the pregnancy you'll have many choices to make throughout the pregnancy and birth and the more information you can gather, the better equipped you are to make these decisions. Read books and contact your GP for advice and support.

Childcare provision in universities varies greatly around the country. Make arrangements with your tutors and lecturers so they can help you organise your timetable to cover all your work. Ask your students' union about where to go to find out about the extra benefits you can claim.

What are the risks of catching a sexually transmitted disease?

An active sex life carries health risks unless you take precautions. Sexually transmitted diseases (STDs) can spread quickly in a community that's not aware of the implications. Always consider contraception and safe sex together (see page 133). Remember, the best protection against STDs is a condom.

Sexually transmitted diseases are spread between both men and women through vaginal intercourse, anal sex or oral sex. The most serious, HIV, is also spread through blood. Here are some particularly high risk activities to avoid for the sake of you and your partner:

○ unprotected penetrative intercourse

○ sharing needles to inject drugs

○ anal intercourse, which is very risky because the lining of the rectum is thinner than that of the vagina and can be ruptured more easily

○ unprotected sex with an infected woman during her period, which increases the risk of contracting HIV by a factor of three.

How do I protect myself?

You only have to have sex once with an infected partner to contract an STD and this includes AIDS. So it's vital that you protect yourself and your partner. The best way to do this is to use a condom. If somebody tries to persuade you that it isn't necessary to use a condom, point out that they're risking their health as well as yours and refuse to sleep with them. You can't tell by looking at someone whether they are infected or not and the risk doesn't diminish the more times you sleep with them.

Oral sex is fairly safe unless one or both of you has cuts in your mouth, then there's a slight risk. But you can get non-lubricated, flavoured condoms to protect you. You're completely safe to kiss, providing neither of you has cuts or sores in your mouth, massage each other, embark on mutual masturbation, share a shower and share sex toys, providing they are washed before your partner uses them.

So, if you're going to have penetrative sex, use a condom. Otherwise experiment with all the safe and sexy things you and your partner can enjoy together.

How would I know if I had an STD?

You may have an STD if you notice:

O unusually coloured discharge or leakage from your penis

O unusual discharge from your vagina in terms of colour, odour or viscosity, possibly causing irritation

O sores or blisters around the penis, anus or vagina

O rash or irritation around the penis, anus or vagina

O a burning sensation or pain when you pee

O a need to pee more frequently

O pain when you have sex.

Some STDs cause only temporary discomfort, but others damage your health permanently. The symptoms can take time to develop, so if you think you've been exposed to any kind of risk don't have sex again until you've been checked out by your doctor, family planning clinic or a specialist genito-urinary medicine (GUM) clinic, also known as a sexual health clinic. You can get a list of local clinics from your GP or the Yellow Pages, listed under 'clinics'. Counselling is also available at these clinics.

Don't be embarrassed if you think you have a sexually transmitted disease – it can happen to anyone who's sexually active, particularly if you have unprotected sex. Here are some of the more common STDs and their symptoms.

Cystitis

Cystitis causes pain when you pee; you feel you need to pee more often and your pee is cloudy or red. It can be caused by friction during sex, but can also be an allergic reaction. It's extremely common in women and less common in men, where it is more likely to be the result of an STD than an allergy. Usually, drinking lots of water and staying away from alcohol and coffee will clear it up in a couple of days. If not, see your GP for a course of antibiotics.

Thrush

Thrush causes itchy vaginal discharge and/or a thick, lumpy discharge in women, while the ends of men's penises become red and sore and they may get little white spots. Bacteria are responsible for thrush and you can get thrush of the mouth, vagina or stomach. Again, it is not necessarily caused by sex. You can buy creams and pessaries from a chemist, but if you have thrush for more than a few days, or if it keeps coming back, then see your GP.

Chlamydia

Bacteria also cause this STD, which produces vaginal discharge or extra moisture in the vagina, a slight leaking of a cloudy fluid from the top of the penis and pain when you pee. It is passed on through vaginal or anal sex. If you don't have this STD treated with antibiotics then it can cause infertility. Make sure your partner(s) are treated too as they could pass it back to you or on to others.

Gonorrhoea

Women rarely experience any symptoms at all but may well be infected if they have had unprotected sex with a man who has gonorrhoea. Men's symptoms will be a burning pain when they pee, a discharge from the penis and irritation and discharge from the anus. Even though a woman may not show any symptoms she will still needed to be treated, so men must tell their partners if they are diagnosed.

Genital warts

Genital warts appear around the vagina, penis and anus and are passed on during penetrative sex. They are caused by a virus and can take a few weeks to a year to appear. Your GP or GUM clinic can give you a cream to treat them, although the virus may remain for a while.

Genital herpes

Genital herpes is also caused by a virus; some people have just one attack, while others have recurring attacks. It causes small clear blisters around the penis, vagina or anus, which burst leaving a very sore area. The blisters are extremely infectious, so don't have sex. Not even condoms provide total protection against genital herpes when the blisters are out or burst. In between attacks of blisters you may still carry the virus around in your body but are unlikely to be infectious. However, always use a condom to be on the safe side.

Pubic lice (crabs)

These small lice can be spread by close body contact such as sharing bedding or towels and through sex. They can cause irritation but are easily treated by lotions available from chemists.

HIV and AIDS

The most life-threatening of all sexually transmitted diseases is that caused by the Human Immunodeficiency Virus (HIV). This can develop into full-blown AIDS, or Acquired Immune Deficiency Syndrome, for which there is no known cure although there are treatments that can keep it in check. The HIV virus is spreading faster among heterosexuals than in any other section of society. HIV and AIDS can affect you, whoever you are. Always take precautions.

The HIV virus is transmitted through blood, semen, vaginal fluids and breast milk. For a person to become infected these fluids have to pass directly into the bloodstream in sufficient quantities – the HIV virus does not survive for long outside the body. There is no risk of catching HIV from everyday social activities such as kissing, sharing crockery, cutlery or food, shaking hands, hugging, swimming in public pools, using public loos, sneezing or coughing.

Should I take an AIDS test?

This is a choice only you can make and if you think there is a possibility that you've contracted the HIV virus, then go for counselling before you make the decision. GUM clinics (listed in the Yellow Pages under 'clinics') have counsellors who can talk to you.

You may want to consider having an AIDS test before you enter a long-term relationship if you and your partner don't want to continue using condoms. However, you have to be sure that you and your partner won't have unprotected sex outside the relationship. Don't believe anybody who says they have an AIDS test before each new relationship unless they provide some kind of proof.

Is there a big student drugs scene?

University is a time when you are likely to come into contact with drugs. As with anything else, don't be pressurised into doing anything you don't want to. If you're tempted to experiment then find out all the facts first. The websites listed in *Lifesavers* can provide further information and advice.

'The student drug scene is nowhere near as big as it is cracked up to be. I have seen students use illegal substances, but I'd seen that before I came to university. Amongst friends I don't really react, it's their choice and as long as I don't think they are developing a problem I will leave them to make their own decision. However, as an elected Students'

141

Union Officer if I see anyone on SU premises using an illegal substance it's an entirely different situation.'

Andrew Stephenson, third-year business management student, Royal Holloway College, University of London

Class A drugs

These are the drugs that carry the highest maximum prison sentences – seven years and a fine for possession and life plus a fine for trafficking.

Ecstasy or MDMA, a common drug on the student scene, is usually produced in the form of a white, yellow, pink or brown tablet. It gives users a surge of energy and the effects can last for several hours. However, it can also lead to feelings of extreme paranoia and insomnia, particularly if you take it when you're feeling unsure about yourself, not getting on with the people you are with, or somewhere you're not comfortable.

Ecstasy has not been around long enough for its long-term effects to be known and has caused a small number of deaths. As with all stimulants, it's more dangerous for people with high blood pressure, epilepsy or heart conditions. It's also impossible to tell what's in an ecstasy tablet – you could be taking ecstasy mixed with anything from heroin to cleaning powders.

The most common hallucinogenic drugs are magic mushrooms and LSD (acid). Magic mushrooms grow wild in many parts of the country and, although it's not illegal to pick them and eat them raw, drying them out could result in a criminal charge. LSD is manufactured illegally in minute quantities which are impregnated into small pieces of blotting paper. The effect of hallucinogens varies according to your surroundings and whether you feel happy and comfortable or not. Inexperienced users may feel very disoriented and confused and all users may experience 'flashbacks', where the trip is relived afterwards. If you're worried about someone in this state then stay with them and, if the feelings don't pass, call a doctor.

Cocaine produces feelings of strength and confidence. However, you can quickly build up a tolerance to cocaine and therefore it's addictive. Regular users may start to feel depressed and ill. If you're tempted, never, ever inject.

Crack is a derivative of cocaine but is highly addictive. The 'high' only lasts a few minutes and is followed by deep depression. Frequent users may have hallucinations and suicidal feelings. Don't touch it.

Heroin produces feelings of relaxation and happiness leading to deep drowsiness and unconsciousness. Tolerance builds up quickly so higher and higher doses are needed. It usually comes in an impure form, making injecting very hazardous and it's extremely difficult to give up.

Class B drugs

Class B drugs carry maximum penalties of five years' imprisonment for possession and 14 years for trafficking. You can be fined for each offence.

Cannabis, also known as dope, grass or hash, is the most commonly used drug on the student scene. It gives users a heightened sense of colour and sound. Like alcohol, it impairs co-ordination so don't drive or operate machinery after smoking it and be extra careful when crossing roads. It has no specific addictive properties but people can become psychologically dependent on it for relaxation or enjoyment. While supply still carries the class B penalties, the laws governing possession are in the process of being reduced to class C, basically meaning that you are likely to be cautioned for possession rather than arrested.

Amphetamine, commonly known as 'speed', is the most commonly used illegal stimulant. It gives you a heightened sense of energy but can have some nasty side effects, such as insomnia, loss of appetite and uncomfortable itching which can lead to anxiety or paranoia. Some people feel unwell for a long time when they stop taking speed after continuous use.

For information and advice about drugs, details of publications and counselling services ring the **National Drugs Helpline** on freephone 0800 77 66 00.

What about legal drugs?

Tobacco and alcohol are legal drugs, providing the age restrictions are obeyed. They are also the most socially acceptable drugs but can be highly addictive and damaging to your health.

The best thing you can do to improve your health is to stop smoking. The benefits of not smoking start the moment you put out your last fag. Within a few months your lung capacity increases significantly and after several years your chances of getting cancer return to those of a non-smoker. However, university is often the time when people become addicted to cigarettes as, free from the constraints of living at home, their consumption increases. The more you smoke, the more damage you do to your health and the more difficult it is to give up. For ideas about ways to stop smoking call **Quitline** on freephone 0800 002200 or visit www.quit.org.uk

---

'I remember going in to town at the weekend and seeing new bars everywhere. On one hand it's really good to have a developing city and it does provide more choice for the consumer. But the negative side is that these types of bars are primarily aimed at students by offering lots of really cheap drinks. This could be seen as encouraging people to drink and spend more than they should on alcohol.'

Andy Bridges, third-year music technology and audio system design student,
Derby University

The current recommended maximum weekly allowance of alcohol is around 21 units for men and 14 units for women. This equates to 10 pints of normal-strength beer or lager for men and seven pints for women. Alternatively, if you drink spirits, men should not drink more than 21 single measures and women more than 14. Regularly drinking in excess of this means you're putting a great deal of strain on your liver, brain, heart and nervous system.

Because alcohol is so much a part of the social scene in all walks of life it's often very difficult to refuse when somebody offers to buy you a drink. This is especially true in the first few weeks of university when you're desperately trying to fit in and don't want to appear 'square'. However, a slight loss of face is preferable to forcing yourself to do something you don't want to do.

If you are going out for an evening where you will be drinking then make sure that you take certain precautions.

○ If eating isn't in your plans then make sure that you eat a meal before you go out so that the alcohol won't be absorbed straight into your stomach lining.

○ Pace yourself. Don't gulp your drinks down and rush to the bar for a refill. Drinking quickly can mean that you get drunk very rapidly without realising it and need to be taken home before the evening has got going. Try and encourage everyone to keep pace with the slowest drinker in the group.

○ Drink plenty of water. It's best to drink water while you are drinking alcohol but if you can't manage that make sure you drink plenty of water before you go to bed. Alcohol dehydrates you and dehydration is one of the reasons you feel so bad after an excessive night.

Remember that alcohol means that you are less able to look after your safety. Try and stick in a group. Don't be tempted to take that two-mile walk back home on your own (see also *Travelling around and staying safe,* Chapter 7)

'I think it's fine to get drunk as long as you are with your friends and it's always useful to have one person who is sober to look after the others. It does shock me when I see people walking home at night when they are really drunk and staggering towards the road and they're alone! I can see why the police and ambulance staff get frustrated with the amount of time and resources that drunken students take up. At every function organised in my halls there has been an ambulance called for someone who has had too much to drink.'

Katherine Lawrey, fourth-year Hispanic studies and history, Birmingham University

You can get information and advice about your own drinking or that of someone you know between 9am and 11pm Monday to Friday and 6pm to 11pm at weekends by calling **Drinkline** on freephone 0800 917 8282.

What if I have problems adjusting to student life?

'The first year is the hardest in some ways because everything is new and unusual. I was quite shy and so I spent most of my time working – unlike most people! In the second year I moved into a house with some friends and I preferred that because it was a lot more homely and I got on well with my housemates.'

Phil Pearce, fifth-year business studies student, Luton University

There are two key pieces of advice welfare officers round the country give to new students coping with living and learning away from home. The first is not to be embarrassed about admitting to any problems you might have – welfare advisers and sabbatical officers (both found in the students' union) have encountered them all before. Secondly, don't feel inferior if it seems that everyone else is handling the transition well – they're probably thinking exactly the same thing about you. So, if you experience difficulties there's a network of people who will deal with your problems in the strictest confidence. Don't just sit and suffer in silence.

Everybody's experience of leaving home and starting university is different but most people have a few problems adjusting. Anyone who claims never to have had a second thought about the whole process is probably lying. The important thing to remember is that you're not alone.

Avoid as many problems as possible by preparing well beforehand (see *Finding somewhere to live*, Chapter 2 and *Living on your own*, Chapter 3). If you've spent time thinking about what you need to take and checked that your accommodation is habitable and available then you're likely to have a much smoother transition.

'The biggest problem initially was not having someone you know to turn to in a difficult situation – either a personal one or when you have problems with your course. You are assigned tutors for that purpose but they appeared quite distant and it didn't seem very clear who I could turn to. But that is a problem only at the beginning, you soon get to know lots of people.'

Jennifer Hogan, fourth-year natural sciences student, Clare College, Cambridge University

What happens if I'm lonely?

There is an old student adage which says that you spend your second two terms trying to lose the friends you made in the first few weeks. This is bound to be true of some people because you're surrounded by so many strangers, so don't worry if you feel you have nothing in common with the first people you meet.

'I barely see the people I spent the first week with now, they weren't the kind of friends you settle with. I did meet loads of people though.'

Susanna Craig, first-year politics and parliamentary studies student, Leeds University

It's very easy, especially in the first few days, to look around and believe that everyone has known each other for years. This is obviously not the case. All first years are in exactly the same boat and those people who appear to be completely at ease are probably thinking that you look pretty cool too.

'If you smile and say hello to someone and they smile and say hello back then you've made a friend. Even if it is just a friend to whom you just smile and say hello. Some people will do more than smile and say hello and you'll have made a friend to go to the bar with or for a coffee.'

**Mona Lisa Cook, former Welfare Officer,
Loughborough University**

Don't worry if you don't get any further than the typical freshers' questions in the first few weeks: What's your name? Where do you come from? What A levels did you do? What course are you on? Talk to any student, past or present, and they'll recognise those questions. They're what all first-year students have in common and are as good a starting point as any other. Use them if you're unsure about how to strike up a conversation.

If you find it difficult to make friends there are steps you can take to make things easier. Don't run home every weekend, but give yourself a chance to mix with your university peers. Stay in touch with the friends you have at home and invite them to come and stay with you at university. You may find it easier to join in university events if you have someone with you. Join a university club where you'll meet people with similar interests. If you find it daunting to walk into a crowded place like a bar or dining room on your own then try meeting people in smaller social situations, like the communal kitchen. Don't take your coffee back to your room but sit in the kitchen with some reading and you'll meet the next person who comes in to make coffee – not a bad icebreaker.

'What helped me adjust was joining sports clubs, like canoeing, which I've done since the first year, where I've met lots of great people and really enjoyed myself.'

**William Wilson, fourth-year management student,
Aston University**

Finally, there are people who just like to be alone and there's absolutely nothing wrong with this. Solitude is only a problem if it makes you unhappy.

What happens if I'm sure I've made a mistake?

Don't make any hasty decisions, but if you realise that you've done the wrong thing by coming to university then there's no point in staying somewhere where you're unhappy. Talk to a welfare adviser or sabbatical officer in the students' union. They'll help identify the cause of the problem and offer advice. If, after talking to people and considering their suggestions, you decide that you still want to leave, then make sure you're aware of the financial implications (see *Can I change course?* page 122).

Can my students' union help?

Students' unions have direct, often personal, experience of the problems facing their students. Sabbatical officers have recent experience of being a student at your particular university and combine this with professional training they've received. They can advise you on any problem you might encounter, from financial, accommodation and educational difficulties to sexual, emotional and health worries. Professional counsellors employed by students' unions are also chosen because of their experience in dealing with student problems.

Many students' unions also run student nightline services. These are telephone helplines run and staffed entirely by students during the evening. They're great at sorting things out, from how to get home if you're stranded in the middle of nowhere to what you should do because nobody spoke to you tonight. The telephone numbers are posted round the university or you can get details of your nearest branch from **Students' Nightline – National Coordinators** at www.nightline.niss.ac.uk

If you don't want to talk to someone at university then the **Samaritans** run a 24-hour helpline which provides a listening ear every day of the year. Call them on 08457 90 90 90, email jo@samaritans.org or visit www.samaritans.org.uk Calls cost no more than a local phone call.

How can the university help?

You can go to your **personal tutor** with any problems you have – not just worries about your course. Tutors know that your course often suffers first if you have other problems, and are interested in helping you sort things out so that you can concentrate on your degree again. The sooner they know, the quicker they can put in place any arrangements to help you, such as giving you some time off or extending deadlines. If you don't tell them they may assume that you're just being lazy or aren't interested in the course.

Lifesavers

Your students' union or university welfare department should be the first point of contact if you have any problems settling into student life as they have experience of dealing with specific student-related issues. They can also help on a range of health matters. However, the following organisations can help with specific problems.

'If there is a group for people with the same special needs as you then join because you can find out how others cope. You may not think that you have a big difficulty but if there is support available to you from others, you should take it.'

**Claire Baldwin, third-year history student,
Aberystwyth University**

If you have any special needs then you should ask your GP to put you in touch with support groups close to your university. It will be useful to know a group of people who know the area with whom you can share your experiences. If you have any difficulty tracking support groups down then contact **Skill** (listed in *Money, money, money*, Chapter 1).

NHS Direct is a helpline and online information service which can advise on all health matters. The helpline is staffed by nurses and if you have any concerns about your health, or that of those close to you, you can ring them up 24 hours a day, seven days a week. An operator will make a note of your name and number and brief details of your concern and give you a time when a nurse will ring you back to talk to you directly. Call **NHS Direct** on 0845 4647 or visit www.nhsdirect.nhs.uk

There's lots of general information about drugs, sex and relationships, managing money, housing, money, careers and legal advice from **the Site's** website at www.thesite.org

There are also tips and information on things like surviving your first week at www.bbc.co.uk/radio1/essentials/students

Chapter 7
Travelling around
and staying safe

So you're used to getting from A to B at home. You even feel confident and safe while travelling around late at night. But what's it going to be like in an area you don't know? How are you going to know which areas you should avoid? And what about travelling abroad – who's got the best deals and where will you stay? Most importantly, how are you going to get  to university in the first place? This chapter answers all these questions and more. For tips on travel and safety, read on.

How will I get to university?

Persuading a parent or friend to give you a lift to university is definitely the best option. Don't worry about losing 'street cred' by having your parents drop you off as most people will be in the same position. If you have to travel to university on public transport then be careful about what you take and how you pack it (see *What should I take with me?*, page 74). Contact the bus, train or coach company a month before you have to travel. Interrogate them thoroughly about the cheapest way you can get there. Most will have Apex and Super Apex fares which are much cheaper than buying tickets on the day. Also ask about the luggage arrangements or limitations. For instance, you can't take bikes on some train routes and there's often a luggage limit on coaches. You may need to arrange to have your belongings delivered to university by a courier company such as Red Star (listed in the phone book).

If you have a lot of things to carry then plan your journey very carefully and allow plenty of time, particularly if it involves changes. What is normally a leisurely five-minute stroll across a platform can be quite a different matter when you try to do this laden down like a pack mule, so avoid short connection times. Also remember that you have to get from the station to the university. Don't leave yourself stranded in a strange area with no idea about how you're going to get there. Phone the university beforehand and get details about how to get there from the station you'll be arriving at, including the cost of a taxi, as this may be a worthwhile investment.

How will I travel around when I'm at university?

'I go everywhere on foot. I don't live on a campus but I still find it easier to walk. It also doesn't cost anything. I sometimes borrow my friends' bikes as I've never actually got round to buying my own.'

**Rob Lucas, third-year critical fine art practice student,
Brighton University**

One of the first things to do when you arrive at university is to find out about the cheapest form of local travel. The methods open to you depend on where you're studying. If you study in a small town then your feet or a bicycle are likely to be the best method of getting you from A to B, whereas if you study in a city then you'll soon become familiar with the public transport networks. However you choose to travel it's going to be a large but essential chunk of your monthly budget (see *How do I make the pennies stretch?*, page 34). Your students' union or the local station will be able to give you local travel details and ticket prices.

Full-time students in London, for example, can get at least a third off tube, bus, tram and Dockland Light Railway travel passes with a student photocard. You need to pick up an application form from your university. The pass costs £5 and you need a passport photo which has been stamped and signed by someone from your university. Further details are on the application form or tel: 020 7918 3935.

'At the beginning I had never travelled alone to London before or used the tube but after I'd done it a couple of times it was OK.'

**Vicky Spencer, third-year textile design student,
Chelsea College of Art and Design**

Many students find that a bike is a cheap and effective way of getting around and most towns now include cycle tracks in their urban developments. The maintenance for a bicycle is much cheaper than for a motorbike or a car and cycling helps keep you fit too. Unless you study in very rural areas it probably isn't worth taking a car to university. The tax, insurance (which may be more expensive for your university town than your home area), MOT, servicing and petrol will be a very big chunk of your not very large budget and you may well find yourself inundated with requests for chauffeur services. If you do ferry friends around you're allowed to accept payment to help cover your costs, but you need a licence to taxi people for profit. Without a licence your insurance is invalid. You won't have this problem if you own a motorbike but, unless you can maintain it yourself, the upkeep will probably be more expensive than using public transport.

If you do take your own transport to university then you'll need to make storage and security arrangements before you leave home.

'I use a car. I'm lucky because my parents pay my car insurance and I worked out that the price of petrol is about the same as buying bus tickets all the time unless you get a bus pass. But I find it much more convenient with a car, especially since this year I'm not living on campus. And if I want to drink one evening I can just take the bus.'

Phil Marsh, second-year engineering student,
Warwick University

University travel schemes

Some students' unions run their own transport schemes. These vary wildly and can range from a women's minibus service late at night, to deals with local taxi firms for students stranded with no means of getting home. Your students' union will advertise such schemes during freshers' week, so look out for details.

'I usually walk everywhere. There is a university hopper bus that can take you between the branch of the campus that's close to my flat and the main campus, but it's always really busy. Some people have bikes which I would recommend, but I just happen to prefer walking.'

Andrew Newsome, first-year maths and computer science student,
Nottingham University

Getting away from university

Reducing the number of times that you travel away from university is one of the ways you can save money. However, going away doesn't always have to break the bank. Check university noticeboards or intranets where you can sometimes find offers of lifts to major cities or events. Invest in a Student Coachcard (£9) offered by National Express Coaches (www.gobycoach.com 08705 80 80 80) and a Young Person's Railcard (£18) (www.youngpersons-railcard.co.uk 08457 48 49 50). These give about a third off all your journeys and both last for a year. They are available from local coach and mainland rail stations. You'll need to take a passport-sized photograph and proof of your age or student status with you.

And if I want to travel abroad?

The years at university are often the only time when people have the freedom to explore far-flung climes. However, it is also the time when this has to be done on a very strict budget. The travel operators have picked up on this and the competition is fierce for student discount fares. Always shop around for the best quote.

'I am looking on the internet for cheap flights as I am planning a trip to Madrid with friends at the moment. It's cheaper to fly at certain times of the year so we buy tickets during the cheaper months. There are also travel agents that work with the university to provide cheap tours for students in places like Italy and Germany. You go in a group and it is cheaper.'

**Sukanta Chowdhury, first-year MBA in finance student,
Luton University**

Before you travel anywhere there are two things you should do. One is to purchase a travel book that covers the country or countries you want to visit. Try either the *Rough Guides* or *Let's Go* guides as these give information about the things you need to do before you travel and local information for when you're there. Then visit your nearest student travel shop; some students' unions have one on site or try the phone book. Student travel shops are the best source of advice on the various student discounts available.

Who should I book a flight with?

The two largest student travel companies are Campus Travel and STA Travel, but look in the phone book or ask other students as there may be alternative student travel companies in your area. If you want to travel by plane then no student has to pay the full fare. There are always discounts available, particularly if you enquire well in advance. There are also specific youth discounts, if you're under 26, and discounts for full-time students, which you're entitled to if you have an International Student Identity Card (ISIC). An ISIC card (£6) also entitles you to discounts on entry to international museums and cinemas, though some discounts may only be available to full-time students under 30. However, an ISIC card also entitles you to reduced cost long-distance phone calls, free email and voice mail, commission-free currency exchange and access to the 24-hour emergency ISIC helpline, which you can call from any part of the world by reversing the charges. So if you have a medical, legal or accommodation emergency, help is just a phone call away.

'I went to STA Travel and got flights for Malaysia which weren't exactly cheap but were cheaper than they would have been otherwise. I also use the internet to find cheap flights and when I got my ISIC card they sent me information about how to get discounts with the card.'

Rhian Jones, fourth-year European studies and French student, Manchester University

---

You can also reduce air costs by taking a courier flight. This is where companies pay a significant proportion of your flight in return for the use of some of your luggage space. However, the company using you as a courier sets your arrival and departure times and these may not fit in with your travel plans. All information about courier flights can be found in *The Courier Air Travel Handbook* by Mark Field at £9.14, published by Perpetual Press. And you can find details of cheap flights at www.aircourier.co.uk

Whichever travel company you book through, always check to see if it is a member of the Association of British Travel Agents (ABTA) and if it isn't don't book a flight with it. ABTA acts as a guarantor for all agents registered with it, so if the travel company fails to supply the goods your expenses should be refunded.

Who should I book through if I want to go by train?

Travelling by train might be a more viable option on your budget. You can get an Inter-Rail card, allowing you to travel for a set period of time through 26 countries divided into 'zones' in Europe and the Mediterranean. A one-month, all-zone card costs £229 if you're under 26. You can buy it from any major national rail station, through a student travel agent or online by visiting www.railchoice.co.uk where you can also find out about other rail discount cards.

What about travelling by coach?

If you can cope with being in a confined space for a long time then a coach ticket is much cheaper than going by plane or rail. But budget for food as you'll have to pay for your food and accommodation if it isn't a sleeper coach en route. You can get tickets for the licensed Eurolines company from any National Express agent. There are unlicensed companies that will be cheaper but they might not follow all the safety laws that govern licensed companies. For more information and to book online visit www.gobycoach.com

The hitchhikers' guide

If you think that hitching is the only way you can afford to travel then be mindful of the security risks involved. Women should never hitch alone. You should also find out about the laws which govern hitching abroad so you avoid hassles with the local police. Different countries have different hitching codes, so ask what code operates where you are. If you use the thumb signal in some countries you'll actually be giving prospective lifts the equivalent of the V-sign, which isn't the best way to encourage people to pick you up. Check a travel guide for the etiquette that applies to the country you are visiting.

Where can I stay when I'm travelling?

If you haven't got a string of relatives and friends across the globe – and most people haven't – then you'll probably end up staying in a mixture of different types of accommodation. Below is a selection of the ones that are most likely to be within your budget.

> 'The best way of staying somewhere cheaply is to sort out the accommodation once you arrive there, which is what we did when we went to Greece this summer. There are always lots of people advertising accommodation at the airport and it's cheaper than sorting it out from over here.'
>
> Katrina Woods, second-year sociology student,
> Ulster University

Youth hostels

Youth hostels are cheap but vary considerably in the rules they enforce. Some will have a certain time by which you have to be back and will expect you to help out with the chores. You may also be expected to sleep in single-sex dorms. Others are more lenient and allow men and women to share a single room, don't lock the doors at a certain time and allow you to cook your own meals. The independent hostels, rather than those run by the Youth Hostelling Association, tend to be the ones that have fewer rules, but shop around to find the ones that best suit your needs.

Find out more about what's available, how you can join the YHA and book hostel places both in the UK and overseas online by contacting:

Youth Hostel Association – *Trevelyan House, Matlock, Derbyshire DE4 3YH. Tel: 0870 870 8808.* www.yha.org.uk

You can also book hostels through the Scottish Youth Hostel Association www.syha.org.uk, Hostelling International Northern Ireland www.hini.org.uk, Hostelling International www.iyhf.org.uk and the large unofficial site www.hostels.com Or you can pick up a copy of *International Youth Hostel Handbook*, volume 1 (Europe) and volume 2 (the rest of the world) published by the YHA, £8.50 each.

Pensions

Pensions are cheap hotels, and you don't usually have to meet any particular criteria in order to stay there. You can stay in a single or shared room. The facilities vary, though, and pensions often don't provide meals, so shop around. They can be very convenient and are often situated in the centre of town.

Hotels

While hotels in the UK may be well over your budget they can be a bargain abroad, so don't dismiss them because you think they'll be out of your league. In Eastern Europe, Asia and Africa in particular, hotels are very cheap when judged by Western European standards.

Under the stars

Camping is a good, cheap form of accommodation while travelling. However, remember that some campsites are a fair distance from the town centre, which might be a problem if local public transport isn't good. If you're travelling the countryside, though, this is not a problem and you can end up in some really beautiful areas.

Sleeping on beaches or in railway stations is obviously a free option, but be careful that you're not robbed during the night. Thieves are very adept at taking your rucksack out from under you while you sleep. If you're Inter-Railing, kill two birds with one stone by arranging to travel to your next destination on an overnight train. Again, watch out for your luggage and make sure you wake up in time if your destination is not the last one on the line.

Can I work while I travel?

'I used the bits of my student loan that I could save to fund my travelling but I also combined work with travel. I've been to Canada with BUNAC, who organised my work visa, and I found a job in the Rocky Mountains. I went to Slovenia on an exchange programme for science students called IAESTE – there I spent 10 weeks at a physics research institute and received a living allowance, which funded my weekend trips to the seaside! I've also been cycling around Iceland and Inter-Railing. Travelling doesn't need to be expensive – there are a lot of scholarships and travel funds about. And working abroad during your holidays can sometimes even allow you to make a profit.'

Jennifer Hogan, fourth-year natural sciences student, Clare College, Cambridge University

You can afford more comfortable travel and accommodation if you earn money while you're abroad. There are many ways of doing this – from participating in well-established schemes such as those run by BUNAC or Camp America to organising your own vacation work. Ask your students' union for details of schemes that your university participates in or get hold of a copy of *Summer Jobs Abroad: 2002* published by Vacation Work at £9.99 or *Work Your Way Round The World* also by Vacation Work at £12.95.

BUNAC organises working holidays for students round the world and arranges flights, visas and support:

BUNAC – 16 Bowling Green Lane, London EC1R 0BH. Tel: 020 7251 3472. www.bunac.org.uk

Camp America finds staff for American children's summer camps after which you can travel for up to 10 weeks:

Camp America – 37a Queen's Gate, London SW7 5HR. Tel: 020 7581 7373. www.campamerica.co.uk

Checklist for travelling abroad

○ Invest in a *Rough Guide* or *Let's Go* guide for the country/ countries you'll be travelling in.

○ Invest in a good quality rucksack.

O Make sure your passport is valid for the duration of your holiday!

O Check with the relevant embassy to see if you need a visa or by logging on to the Foreign Office's site at www.fco.gov.uk

O Take out adequate travel insurance.

O Make sure you've had all the necessary injections (ask your doctor).

O Take some basic medicines with you, including sun cream and mosquito repellent spray.

O Take a toilet roll.

O Check the availability of contraception as you can't always buy condoms over the counter.

O Invest in a good quality penknife.

O Take a travel alarm clock.

O Carry all money in a money belt under your clothes.

O In some countries it's better to have US dollars, so you may want to take traveller's cheques in dollars and some dollars in cash.

O Don't take too many clothes with you. Just make sure you have something waterproof, something warm and something cool, something to protect you from the sun and a very comfortable pair of boots or shoes.

O Don't pack your rucksack too full as you may want to collect things on the way.

O Don't take anything valuable with you. Leave your jewellery and watch at home.

O If camping, check your tent before you leave – it may be too late to get more tent pegs when you're there. Also take a mallet and roll mats.

O Take a sleeping bag even if you're not camping.

'I like travelling because I feel independent and far away from everything. I am able to control what I do each day. And obviously you are also seeing different cultures and broadening your horizons.'

Jeremy Carlton, PhD biochemistry student,
Bristol University

How do I keep safe?

Wherever or however you travel, safety is something both men and women should be aware of. This is particularly so when you first arrive at university or are travelling in an area you don't know, as the risks are greater when you are not familiar with an area. Fortunately, violent attacks are rare, but statistics do show that it is young men who are most at risk. If you're attacked it's vital that you report it immediately to the police, where you can also receive support.

You may feel more confident if you take a self-defence course, where you'll be taught to avoid dangerous situations and protect yourself should you be attacked. Ask your students' union if it runs one or call your local police station for details.

'I have taken up Tai Kwondo, mainly because I feel that Coventry (the nearest big city) isn't particularly safe so I feel happier having taken it up.'

Phil Marsh, second-year engineering student,
Warwick University

How can I avoid danger?

The best way to stay safe is to try and make sure that you travel around in a group – there really is safety in numbers. However, even groups of people can get into trouble, so whenever you are out and about make sure you avoid potentially dangerous situations and stay alert to your surroundings. These safety guidelines apply equally to men and women.

- O Don't take short cuts through unlit or unpopulated areas.
- O Don't dawdle along in a world of your own.
- O Don't listen to your personal stereo.
- O Don't walk close to bushes and hedges.
- O Don't have a regular routine whereby you always walk back at the same time and follow the same route.
- O Don't carry a weapon – it may be used against you.
- O Do stick to well-lit streets.
- O Do be alert and look back occasionally to see if you're being followed.

O Do walk at a brisk pace and purposefully.

O Do carry a personal safety alarm and keep it somewhere accessible.

O Do wear non-restricting clothes and shoes you can run in.

If you're attacked, shout as loudly as you can. Don't scream, as some attackers get a kick out of hearing a victim scream but shout something specific like 'No!' or 'Call the police!'. If you think you're being followed, go to the nearest lit public place or house and ask to use the phone. Only fight back if you can't escape. If you do have to fight back then poking your fingers in your attacker's eyes is effective and unexpected. Stamping on someone's foot or kicking them in the shins will surprise them and may loosen their grip.

'If I am alone I walk in well-lit areas but usually I walk with other people at night. I never walk alone late at night.'

**Rhiannon Michael, second-year law and German student,
Aberystwyth University**

Public transport

If you travel by public transport rather than your own two feet there are additional precautions you can take to protect your safety.

O Don't wait at isolated and empty bus stops and stations.

O Don't get into an empty compartment or one with just one other passenger in it, if you have a choice.

O Don't strike up conversations with strangers or accept any invitations to get off the public transport and for them to walk you home.

O Do sit next to the driver, conductor or, if you're a woman, another woman.

O Do complain to a driver, conductor, guard or other person in authority if you're pestered or made to feel awkward.

O Do make sure you leave plenty of time to catch the last bus, train or tube, particularly if you have connections to make.

Find out whether your students' union runs its own alternative transport. This will often be much cheaper, and definitely safer, than relying on public transport.

Taxis

If you're stranded somewhere late at night rather than try to make it back on foot or public transport, it's safer to take a taxi provided you use a licensed firm. Your safety is worth the price of a cab fare. However, you need to take some precautions when booking or getting into a taxi.

○ Don't take a ride in unmarked cars claiming to be taxis.

○ Do ask mini-cab drivers for their identification or make a note of the black cab number.

○ Do plan well in advance and use a reputable firm.

○ Do ask for a woman driver if you're a woman travelling alone late at night.

Some students' unions run schemes in conjunction with local taxi firms, whereby you can hand over your union card if you haven't got the money to get back home. The firm then invoices the union and you pay when you pick up your card. Ask your students' union whether they have such a scheme.

'If I'm out really late after a night of clubbing I get a taxi back home which takes you door to door, so there is no problem. The last bus is at 11:30pm so I take that if it is not too late.'

William Wilson, fourth-year management student,
Aston University

At home

We all like to think that our home is our castle and once we close the door we're safe and sound. While this is true most of the time, burglars are cunning and you need to make things as difficult as possible for them.

○ Don't hide your keys outside.

○ Don't leave doors and windows open – keep them locked.

○ Don't let bushes or gardens get overgrown as they provide perfect cover for burglars.

○ Don't let strangers in to use the phone – they may be burglars checking for valuables.

○ Don't invite strangers in, even if they say they are a friend of one of your flatmates.

○ Don't tell people who ring that you're alone.

○ Do draw all curtains and blinds.

○ Do fit and use a door chain.

○ Do keep some lights on.

○ Do make sure there is adequate lighting outside the house which illuminates all potential hiding places, like alleyways or corners.

○ Do lock your bedroom door if possible but have the key handy in case you need to get out quickly.

○ Do ask to see identification of any 'officials' who call.

Never enter the house if you notice something unusual – the intruder may still be inside. Call the police immediately. They'd rather have a false alarm than have you risk putting yourself in danger. If your house is broken into or the lock tampered with in any way then get the locks changed immediately.

For more information about protecting your home contact your local police crime prevention desk (at the local police station listed in the phone book) as they'll be more than happy to offer you free advice on how to improve the security of your home.

Date rape drug

There have been a few cases of students having what is termed the 'date rape drug' slipped into their drinks. To avoid this happening to you, don't let strangers buy you a drink and don't leave your drink unattended, which could allow someone to drug it.

If you suspect that you have been the victim of a drug rape then report it immediately to the police, where a specially trained officer will see you. You can also get support, counselling and legal advice from:

Women Against Rape – *PO Box 287, London NW6 5QU. Tel: 020 7482 2496.*

Lifesavers

You can get more information about personal safety at home and abroad, including publications and personal safety alarms from:

Suzy Lamplugh Trust – *PO Box 17818, London SW14 8WW. Tel: 020 8876 0305.* www.suzylamplugh.org

Discounted student flights and accommodation can be booked through:

CTS Travel – *44 Goodge Street, London W1. Tel: 020 7290 0620 (Europe) 020 7290 0621 (Worldwide).* www.ctstravel.co.uk

For details of student discounts, cheaper fares and suggested accommodation for independent travellers visit the STA branch nearest you or contact:

STA Travel – *Head Office, Priory House, 6 Wrights Lane, London W8 6TA. Tel: 0870 1600 599.* www.statravel.co.uk

Discounted air, road and rail travel and accommodation can be booked through:

Travel Cuts – *295a Regent Street, Oxford Circus, London W1B 2HN. Tel: 020 7255 1944 (Europe) 020 7255 2082 (North America and Worldwide).* www.travelcuts.co.uk

For details of student air, road and rail travel and suggestions for accommodation visit your local campus branch or contact:

Usit Campus Travel – *52 Grosvenor Gardens, London SW1W OAG. Tel: 0870 240 1010.* www.campustravel.co.uk

To apply for or update your passport pick up a form from the Post Office which gives the address of your nearest passport office. If you have any questions or if you need a passport urgently, call the **UK Passport Service** advice line on 0870 521 0410 or visit www.passport.gov.uk for details.

Publications

For comprehensive information on any country that you're thinking of visiting, get hold of the relevant guide to that country such as the *Rough Guides* or *Let's Go* guides. They are written in an easy-to-follow style and contain information about what to do before you travel and when you get there.

Chapter 8
Life after university

How will you pay off your student debt? How do you find your ideal company? Can your CV get you a foot in the door and will your covering letter woo? How can you avoid falling flat on your face at interview? Where are jobs advertised? And what if you don't want to enter the world of work immediately?

These days as students leave university owing more money, thinking about what you are going to do after university becomes more important. It might seem too soon to be considering what you will do when you have got your degree under your belt when you've barely had your letter of acceptance. However, your university days can help make you stand out from the crowd if you use them wisely. You will also find this chapter useful if you need to get a job while you study.

What are employers looking for?

Although getting your degree is a fantastic personal achievement you have to remember that each year the number of people who also reach that goal is growing and, worse, they are all looking for jobs at the same time as you are. You need to make sure that you use your time at university to do more than just emerge with a piece of paper. Employers look for interesting, rounded people who can demonstrate initiative and flair. So saying that you just spent every evening sitting in the student bar won't impress.

If you study a degree with a large practical element to it then building up skills which you can demonstrate to an employer is easier but, again, remember that others will have the same qualifications as you. If you follow a degree which is more theoretical, such as history, you need to think about what you might like to do and try and get some practical experience which will help you stand out from the crowd.

'My last job used a lot of what I learnt in my degree, but in the job I have now I am using what I learnt at A level. I know a lot of people who are doing jobs which aren't related to their degrees at all, but I prefer it this way because I don't feel out on a limb – I will at least know the theory even if I don't know the practice.'

Amanda Warburton, microbiology with medical bioscience graduate, Kent University

Careers advisors recommend that you start job hunting at least six months before you are due to graduate. Employers are aware that competition is fierce and expect to see applications from soon-to-be graduates from this time.

What can I do at university?

One of the great benefits of university is that it offers a wealth of opportunities to get involved, try things out and grow your skills. And you can do this while pursuing something that interests you. Join a club or a society (see *Freshers' Week,* Chapter 4) and try to get involved in how it is run. You don't have to have been on any committees at school or have any other experience to do this – all you need is enthusiasm and the willingness to lend a hand.

Playing a team sport will demonstrate to employers that you are a good team member, competitive and physically fit (providing you don't celebrate too hard at the end of each match or training session). However, getting involved in organising matches or sitting on the board that makes budgeting decisions adds some other useful strings to your bow, such as responsibility, decision making, organisational skills and budgeting experience – all very useful in the employment market. The same is true if you get involved with a society, like the drama or film society. Indeed, some societies can provide very useful specific experience if you are looking to work in a particular area. For example, if you would like a job in the media (and there are many students who would) you must get involved with your students' newspaper, radio or TV station. You'll need to demonstrate that you are really interested in the media and have some work you can show prospective employers. Similarly, if you are interested in working in the voluntary sector, then getting involved with your student rag, nightline service or any specific societies which support development issues or community activities will help you get your foot in the door. You can also get involved in running your students' union, which always impresses as it demonstrates leadership skills as well as a raft of organisational abilities, budgeting, marketing, PR experience and the like.

'I got involved in societies focusing and campaigning on development issues, poverty and human rights and this really allowed me to find out more about these issues and where my interests lie. I think getting this kind of experience is really useful – both in terms of finding a job, but also finding out about what kind of work you want to do.'

Amy North, MSc development studies student, London School of Economics, University of London

If you are not sure what you would like to do you can also use clubs and societies to try out things you think you might enjoy. So if you think you might be interested in photography but haven't tried it before then join the photography club! And don't rule out getting involved if you are following a degree which leads you very directly into a particular job, such as medicine. You still have to apply for jobs and someone who has not just dedicated their time to studying will probably stand out. People with heavily timetabled degrees tend to have less time to dedicate to clubs and societies but most manage to find time to pursue some interests and/or sports.

Don't just sit in the union bar every night and waste the opportunities that clubs and societies and your students' union offer. Get out, get involved and get some experience.

What about work experience and placements?

If you can organise work experience or a work placement then this is an excellent way of demonstrating to employers that you have initiative and some hands-on experience. Write to companies you are interested in and ask them whether they run any schemes (see *How to impress with your CV*, page 170 and *Writing a good covering letter*, page 172). Follow it up with a phone call or two but don't harass them! Be prepared to make several enquiries before you find an opportunity. Some companies carry information about schemes on their websites, so do your research first (see also page 182).

'I decided that I was interested in finding out more about working in television so I looked up the websites of the main TV channels and production companies and sent a CV and covering letter to the addresses they gave. I didn't have any experience so I was really pleased when I was finally accepted by one. Although I was in a small department I learnt a lot of things I had no idea about before and I enjoyed myself! I would say that, if you are interested in something, go for it – even if you think you don't stand a chance. Work experience is an essential element of your CV.'

Isabelle Brewerton, fourth-year modern and medieval languages student, Corpus Christi College, Cambridge University

If you get work experience or a placement then make the most of it.

Do:

○ turn up on time smartly dressed

○ be friendly and ask how you can help

○ be sensitive to people's work pressures

○ go to lunch with your colleagues if you are offered the chance – it's a great way to get to know them more informally

○ ask people how they got into the industry and what advice they would give

○ do the work you are given diligently, checking carefully for any errors – if people see that you produce good quality work they may trust you to do something with more responsibilities

○ ask someone in the office to write a short open reference for you.

If you enjoy the experience then ask whether they have any graduate entry schemes and make sure you leave a copy of your CV (see page 171) with the personnel or HR department. It might be worth staying in touch with the people that you have worked with by occasional email to remind them who you are (some companies have a high turnover of work experience people) and that you would be interested in working for the company. But don't bombard them!

Don't:

○ sit in a corner looking bored – even if they haven't got anything for you to do there and then, spend that time doing something which shows you are interested in the company, such as browsing the company intranet or reading any printed material they produce

O sit on the phone to your mates or enter into email exchanges – your friends may be impressed by your new 'job' but it will really annoy your new colleagues

O take long lunches – ask what time everyone else takes lunch and stick to that time too

O talk loudly into the telephone – office background noise is a real irritant.

And if you don't enjoy yourself try to hide your feelings. Even if you are convinced this is not the industry for you, you might come across one of the people in the office again and don't want to get a bad reputation. Or you could end up getting interviewed next time for a job you really want by one of their friends who is already well versed in how much you hated working with their mate.

Doing a sandwich degree or being sponsored by a company will also give you access to work experience and, because you will be with the company for longer, you may be given your own project. This will clearly demonstrate your skills to other employers and provide you with extremely valuable hands-on experience (see also *Could I be sponsored?*, page 25).

What about my part-time job?

These days employers recognise that many students undertake part-time work while they study or during the holidays and this too can provide some useful skills. While every paper round you've ever done might not be impressive you should think carefully about what your part-time job does offer you. Although working in a supermarket or local bar may not be your ideal occupation, you will be learning valuable lessons about dealing with people, handling money, managing difficult situations and being disciplined and organised. Don't think that employers won't be impressed by these skills. Of course, you may be lucky enough to land a job that gives you a foot in the door of your chosen career, like answering the phones at a local radio station or doing administrative shifts at a solicitors' office, but don't worry if the job you do to boost your student loan is working in a local fast-food restaurant. You will be developing skills by doing that job too – you just need to know how to present them.

'I don't think I will use my degree when I graduate. I remember reading in the prospectus before I started my course that most geographers don't use geography in their chosen career but become accountants or something! I'm not saying that's what I will do, but my choice of career won't depend on what I studied at university.'

Allan Jones, third-year geography student,
Lancaster University

How to impress with your CV

Your CV is your introduction to future employers and people who you want to do work experience with. It needs to create a good impression.

Although you'll always hear tales of people lying on their CVs and getting away with it, generally it is a really bad idea. With the internet and databases it is much easier to check facts and you never know how diligent your prospective employers will be in following things up or who they know. And then you risk the utter humiliation of being discovered lying when asked about something you put on your CV to 'pad' it out. Just imagine how many other future employers will get to hear about your embellishments as you become the interviewer's favourite story to dine out on.

It's much better to stick to the facts but present your experience, even if it is limited, in a positive way which emphasises the skills you gained and used. Try to use 'active' words like 'organised' and 'achieved' but avoid using too many 'I did this' phrases. A few can be useful, but too many get in the way of the information. And keep information short and to the point – you don't want to bore the recruiter before they get to the end.

How you organise your CV depends a bit on the experience that you have had. People with a lot of experience may want to organise their CVs according to their key skills but unless you are confident about that format it's best to stick to something more traditional, like the one shown.

Make sure that your CV is clearly typed in at least 11 point font, is free from fancy typefaces, doesn't run to more than two sides of A4 and is clearly printed on good quality paper. You should also avoid too much elaborate formatting, particularly if you need to email your CV. If you have to send it through the post then use a hard-backed envelope so that it doesn't arrive dog-eared.

Joe King

07770 123456
joeking@universitycollegecampus.ac.uk

Holiday contact:
12 Crown Street, London SW2 2ZZ
020 7123 4567

Term-time contact:
Room 22, Building 2, University College Campus, Regent Street, Coventry CV2 2ZZ
024 1234 5678

Personal profile

An enthusiastic finalist with good research and writing skills, a confident communicator and keen team player

Education

2000 to present: University College, Coventry – English and Media Studies (predicted result 2:1)

Modules include twentieth-century English, the development of script to screen and practical units in camera operation and editing. Requires regular group presentations and producing practical work to deadlines.

1993-2000: Scholar School – London

Three A levels: English (A), drama (B) and French (B)

Awarded the sixth form prize for English and was leader of the orchestra
10 GCSEs with four subjects at A* and two at A, including English Language and maths

Work experience

February 2001 to present: University bar tender

A member of the term-time bar staff team responsible for keeping the bar running smoothly even when busy, balancing the tills and dealing face to face with customers. Includes training in stock taking and ordering.

December 2000: Post Office – London

Relief postal worker responsible for sorting mail. Required attention to detail and good organisational skills.

June – August 2000: Local newspaper – London

Two-month work placement in a busy newsroom conducting interviews, researching copy for articles and assisting in running the office, including co-ordinating the section editor's diary.

1998–1999: Deep Kleen Kleeners – London

Saturday shop assistant at local dry cleaning business, responsible for dealing with customers, balancing the tills and organising the shop.

Skills

Excellent research and writing skills honed through practical journalistic experience.

Confident communicator used to dealing with people face to face and on the phone in a great variety of circumstances.

Computer literate in most word processing and email packages, plus Excel and Photoshop. Increasing familiarity with video editing software.

Interests

I follow my interest in journalism by regularly writing for my student newspaper, mainly for the news section.

I play the violin to Grade 8 standard and have joined the university orchestra.

I enjoy travelling and spent a month touring round Greece last summer.

In addition, I enjoy films, particularly historical films, and have recently started learning how to develop black and white photographs.

References available on request

You don't have to include your age, marital status or state of health – it is illegal for employers to discriminate against you on these grounds. Nor should you write Curriculum Vitae across the top of the page. It will be obvious what it is from the layout and you want people to remember the most important detail – your name – so make sure it is at the top.

And finally, check, check and check again. Your CV needs to be 100% accurate. Get a friend to help you, as it's really difficult to spot your own mistakes, then show it to an expert – a careers advisor. Your university should have one. If not, look in the phonebook under 'careers' for details of your nearest one. Careers Offices offer free advice to those under 21 but should be sympathetic to students even if you are older.

'There is a great careers service in Edinburgh – you can go and talk to an advisor and they are really helpful. They take you through your CV and if you have any questions they show you where to look and who to contact.'

Samantha Northey, third-year Chinese student, Edinburgh University

Writing a good covering letter

No CV, however wonderful, should be sent off without a covering letter. A covering letter introduces you and lets the employer know how you heard about them. It should fit easily onto one side of A4 and should run to around four paragraphs.

In the first paragraph state where you saw the job advertised and the title of the job you are applying for, if you are responding to an advertisement. If you are requesting work experience then use the first paragraph to say, briefly, how you know about the company and why you are interested in it.

In the second paragraph elaborate on the skills you can offer them but be careful of just repeating your CV. Instead, focus on specific skills your course or interests have given you and why you think they apply to the job or company.

Then reiterate your interest in the position or company. Finally, sign off with a positive phrase which anticipates them wanting to seeing you, such as 'I look forward to hearing from you'.

Your covering letter should be typed, unless a company specifically requests a hand-written letter, and in the same typeface and font as your CV.

'*After I'd researched the companies I was interested in on the internet I then sent my CV and covering letter to the ones I thought sounded interesting, explaining my interests. When making speculative applications I think it is really important that you use your covering letter to really explain your interests and experience – otherwise you could end up just stuffing the envelopes – although you're bound to have to do this some of the time.*'

**Amy North, MSc development studies student,
London School of Economics, University of London**

Getting application forms right

There are some companies that bypass CVs and covering letters by getting you to fill out an application form. These usually require more work and thought. Make sure that you answer every single question that is asked – even if you write n/a (not applicable) against an answer. This is so that the potential employer knows that you have not just left it out or not spotted it.

The key to filling out a successful application form is sticking to the point. Read the job specification and person specification carefully then make sure that each answer you give on the application form relates to one of the points in the person specification, wherever possible. If you come across a question where your experience doesn't quite fit with the person specification try to make a close match or say that this is an area you are interested in being given the opportunity to develop.

The other tricky thing about application forms is filling them out neatly and getting all that you want to say into the boxes provided. Take many photocopies and do some rough versions until you are happy with what you want to say and are sure that it will fit. Get someone to check your final rough version for errors before you transfer it onto the original – in your best handwriting, using a good quality pen.

Alternatively, you can 'cheat' application forms a bit by mocking up the same-sized boxes on the computer, typing your answers, sticking them into the relevant spaces on the original and then photocopying the final result to send off. This is a bit fiddly but a good idea if your writing is messy. You should also do a couple of trial runs at sticking your answers in before you commit them to the original. The other option for people with messy writing could be to reproduce the form as a word processed document although it's probably best to check with the company first. They may have written references or markings on the form which need to be preserved.

173

What are psychometric tests?

In recent years some companies have been using psychometric tests, which are questionnaires designed to reveal your personality, motivations and career ambitions. The nature of these tests means that companies are looking for 'right' and 'wrong' answers and the best way of preparing for them is to get some practice. You can find examples by putting 'psychometric tests' into an internet search engine or by visiting www.ase-solutions.co.uk. There are also a number of books on the market, such as *How to Master Psychometric Tests* by Mark Parkinson (Kogan Page, £7.99) and *Prepare for Tests at Interview: for graduates and managers* by Robert Williams (ASE, £9.99). You may also be sent practice tests by employers.

Psychometric tests tend to be broken up into three papers – verbal skills, mathematical ability and personality tests. The verbal papers are like language comprehension tests and the more you do the more familiar you will become with the style. Respond to each question by asking yourself, 'Does my answer follow on logically from the information that I have been provided with?' If your maths is a bit dodgy then make sure you swot up on things like percentages, ratios, basic statistics and graphs. And when it comes to the personality tests just be yourself. Don't try to second-guess the answers that the company is looking for – you could end up skewing your personality in the wrong direction! For all papers you should make sure that you read the instructions carefully and then get on with providing your answers. Don't waste time by spending ages agonising over the 'right' answer. With ability tests you are likely to score higher marks the more questions you get through, so make a decision and move on.

You also need a clear head to score highly in psychometric tests, so avoid drinking alcohol the night before and make sure you get a good night's sleep. Eat a good filling breakfast and arrive in plenty of time.

Getting clued up – how to research a company

'I would definitely recommend looking up information about the company which is interviewing you – what they do, what you would be expected to do. I had a really embarrassing interview when I didn't know anything about the company!'

Amanda Warburton, microbiology with medical bioscience graduate, Kent University

Avoid looking like a fool by doing some thorough research on the company – preferably before applying for a job, but certainly before you attend an interview. It's a bit like revising for one of your exams. If you know the history of the company, what it does and what its plans are then you won't get any surprise questions.

The internet is a blessing. Most companies have websites, so visit them and read the information thoroughly. Do an internet search to find out if the company has been in the news recently and why. Pick up trade journals from libraries or careers services to get an idea of the industry in general and to check for recent mentions of the company which is interviewing you.

Some universities run schemes where you can speak to graduates of your university who now work in that company. If your university has this scheme then use it. There's nothing like a personal chat to get you clued up and to give you a true picture of what working for that company is really like. Websites are very useful but they will only give you the 'official' line. And if you get the chance to mention to the interviewers that you have done this you will score big initiative points!

Don't despair if your university doesn't have such a scheme. Try family, friends, parents of friends, their relatives, their friends – you never know who might know someone who is working in that company. Spread the word and see what happens.

'I would say that the best thing you can do in a job interview is to be yourself. I knew about the job that I was applying for and prepared by reading up on the company and the profession.'

**Sarah Brown, maths graduate,
Christ's College, Cambridge University**

Showing confidence – how to handle interviews

The first thing is to look the part. Psychologists estimate that it takes a fraction of a second for someone to make a judgement about you, so it is very important to create a good first impression. If you create a bad impression you have to create five or six good impressions before someone will think differently about you – that's a lot of hard work when you want to be concentrating on answering the questions asked.

So dress smartly. Your student loan may not stretch to a suit, but try to buy or borrow a jacket and wear it with smart trousers or a skirt (if you are a woman and prefer wearing skirts). Make sure that your hair is freshly washed and neat – you should take a brush or comb with you in case you get windswept en route. Avoid carrying any big bags and definitely don't bring your shopping to an interview. It will be difficult to create a good impression if you are struggling in through the door and then searching for somewhere to put everything. If you want or need to take examples of your work then buy or borrow a folder or portfolio.

Plan your route. It may sound extravagant but if you don't know the area where the company is then it is as well to do a 'dummy' run so that you are confident about where you are going and how long the journey will take. Allow plenty of time to get there and take maps with you even if you are fairly sure you know where to find the company. You don't want to add to your pre-interview nerves by fretting about whether you are going to get there on time, and if you're in a panic it's easy to get lost. Sometimes companies send a map out with the interview confirmation letter but take an A–Z as well as these maps are sometimes not very detailed or are awkward to read. And take the confirmation letter with you too. It will tell you where to go, what time you have to be there and, if the receptionist looks blankly at you when you arrive, you'll have your evidence to hand.

'It's a really good idea to plan things like your transport, clothes and so on in advance so that you can be calm and focused on the day.'

**Sarah Brown, maths graduate,
Christ's College, Cambridge University**

Arrive at your interview no later than five minutes before it is due to start. However, you shouldn't arrive too early either – 10 minutes is the maximum. Arriving too early can annoy people who have scheduled you an appointment time and may well be in the middle of interviewing another candidate and don't want to take a call from reception telling them you are here. However, it will often take five minutes for you to go through any required security measures, be met by someone and taken to the room where the interview will take place. You may only have 20 minutes or so to persuade them why you are the correct candidate, so you want to make sure you are in the room bang on time.

Make sure you find out who will be interviewing you in advance and what their position in the company is. If this information isn't in the confirmation letter then ring. This means you won't look blank when you meet them face to face or be distracted by trying to remember who they are and what they do, instead of concentrating on your answers. You may be interviewed by two or even three people.

When you are introduced to them, look them confidently in the eye and give a good firm handshake – this all communicates confidence even if you are shaking in your boots. Be careful not to stare them out or crush their bones though. Smile and say how nice it is to meet them and thank them for seeing you, then sit in the seat indicated and prepare to face their questions.

The more research you have done (see *Getting clued up – how to research a company*, page 174) and the better you have prepared, the stronger chance you will stand. Look back over your application and the details of the job you were sent, think about the questions they might ask and prepare some answers.

'I would say that it is really important to have worked out why you want to do that kind of job and why you would be good at it. It's really important to be positive about and flag up all the relevant experience you have, and show how interested you are in doing that type of work.'

**Amy North, MSc development studies student,
London School of Economics, University of London**

Some standard interview questions include:

O Describe your experience so far. Why do you think you are a good candidate?

O What attracts you to this post?

O What do you think are the key responsibilities of this job and how do they relate to your experience?

O Why should we give this job to you when we have more experienced candidates applying?

O Where do you see yourself in five years' time?

O Do you prefer working as part of a team or taking on your own projects?

O Would you be prepared to work some weekends and evenings?

O What are your strengths and weaknesses?

You may also be asked a 'role play' question where you are presented with a situation you are likely to encounter in the job, such as a tight deadline or apparently conflicting priorities. What interviewers are looking for here is a logical approach to that situation, which

177

demonstrates your understanding of prioritising. There's unlikely to be a 'right' answer they are looking for – they will be more interested in seeing how you think. Occasionally, interviewers use 'trick' questions but, again, this is more to see how you think than because they are expecting you to come up with the definitive answer.

Try to answer each question clearly without rambling, drawing on relevant practical examples to illustrate your skills. Don't forget that your degree will have equipped you with research, writing, presentation and public speaking skills, all of which are invaluable to employers whatever job you are applying for – you can use examples from it too. Don't be afraid of a pause, these are natural in conversation and can allow time for you to gather your thoughts. And do ask for a question to be repeated or rephrased if you don't quite understand it rather than blunder in and try to bluff your way through. Finally, if you really get stumped and don't know the answer it's much better to admit that than lie or stumble an answer. The question may have been a trick one anyway!

Interviews can seem daunting but the key thing to remember is that you are there because you have presented an application that meets their criteria and interests them. They are interested in what you have to say. So try to relax, remember to smile and present the best case you can.

Have some questions lined up at the end of the interview as it demonstrates an interest in the company, but it's probably best not to wade in and ask them how much you will be paid. If salary hasn't been discussed then make sure you ask the question discreetly and amongst other questions so you don't give the impression it is the only thing that interests you. It's as well to have quite a few questions lined up in case they answer the two that you'd thought of during the course of the interview and you might want to have some general questions up your sleeve too.

○ Are there any training opportunities attached to this position?

○ Typically what have people in this post gone on to achieve?

○ What salary range does this position command?

○ How much contact does this department have with other departments?

○ How much contact does this department have with outside clients?

O Is the role mainly office-based or are there opportunities to meet our clients?

O How will you be letting candidates know of your decision?

'Prepare questions to ask them in advance so that when they say 'Do you have any questions?' you don't have an embarrassed silence, and it shows that you are interested.'

Amanda Warburton, microbiology with medical bioscience graduate, Kent University

At the end of the interview, stand up and shake hands, smile and reiterate your interest in the job. Thank them for seeing you and say that you look forward to hearing from them soon.

Then go out and do something that you really enjoy, like meeting friends, seeing a film or playing a sport to take your mind off the interview. There's nothing else you can do now – the decision is in their hands.

How do I decide which job would suit me?

If you are following a course such as medicine, veterinary medicine or law your career can be clearly defined and your course tutors will be able to let you know what the next steps are. For others, though, the decision may not be so clear cut. Some people are so full of trepidation at entering the world of work that they prefer to take temporary positions. That is absolutely fine – in fact, there can be some really interesting temporary positions where people may be prepared to employ you in a role with more responsibilities than if they were employing you long-term.

'I know I will use my degree in my career. Chinese is a very specialised subject, so I want to use it. At the moment I think I would like to go and live in the East for a few years then come back and do a Masters and generally continue studying to get as many qualifications as possible.'

Samantha Northey, third-year Chinese student, Edinburgh University

If you are having difficulties deciding what you want to do then ask yourself some basic questions.

O Would you prefer to work as part of a team or on your own?

O Do you want a job that is office-based or to work outdoors?

○ Would you mind putting in long hours or would you prefer to do something which you have more control over?

○ Would you like a job that involves dealing with people?

○ Would you like a job that involves travel?

○ Do you want to do something where you can progress up the management ladder?

○ Do you want to do something creative?

○ Do you want a job where you can gain professional qualifications?

○ Do you want to work for one company or would you like to work on many different projects as a freelance?

Then make a list of the things that you really enjoy and those skills that you think you have. You don't have to restrict these just to what you have learnt during your degree or the jobs that you've had. Your hobbies and interests may provide some useful clues too and you may just be able to turn them into a career choice. Enlist the help of your family and friends when making this list. They may see strengths (or weaknesses) which you didn't realise you had. However, this only works if they are prepared to be honest and upfront with you.

Armed with this information, go to your university careers service. An advisor there can talk to you about your options and maybe suggest things that you hadn't thought of. If your university doesn't have a careers service then you can find the one closest to you by looking in the phonebook under 'careers'.

Where are jobs advertised?

Once you have narrowed down the types of jobs and areas you are interested in, then you can start your search. Here are the main sources of job adverts, some of which will also be helpful if you are looking for term-time or holiday work.

Graduate recruitment fairs

These are golden opportunities to find out about the sort of companies which want your services. The companies looking to recruit graduates take stalls, where they have company representatives to answer your questions and tell you about the opportunities. Often these representatives will have joined the company the year before as graduate trainees. Make sure you take several copies of your CV so you can leave it with those companies you are interested in. Take away any literature they have available and then make a follow-up phone call to those you are interested in pursuing to enquire about the next steps you should take.

There is a large graduate fair held in London each autumn and some universities also hold their own so ask for details at your students' union or careers service or contact Prospects (listed in *Lifesavers*).

'I went to my university careers service and they gave me a booklet full of details about which companies will be doing presentations. Presentations are very useful because there are representatives from lots of different companies that you can go and talk to.'

Samantha Northey, third-year Chinese student, Edinburgh University

Graduate vacancy bulletins

There are two main graduate vacancy bulletins. *Prospects Today*, published weekly from April to September, carries current vacancies and *Prospects for the Finalist*, published four or five times a year, carries details of openings for students when they graduate. Look in your university library, university careers service or your local careers service, or have vacancies emailed to you from Prospects (see *Lifesavers*).

Newspapers

Most local and national newspapers carry job adverts in addition to weekly careers supplements. Some national newspapers, famously *The Guardian*, carry job adverts that relate to particular fields on specific days of the week so you need to find out when the jobs you want are advertised. There are also 'job finder' papers, predominantly for local areas. Visit your newsagent to get an idea of what's around.

Trade papers and magazines

Some of the best jobs are only advertised in trade papers and magazines as employers want to encourage applications from people who can demonstrate an interest in the area by keeping up with industry news. There are some trade publications, such as *The Stage*, which are the only published way of finding out about upcoming jobs in that field. If you are unsure about which publications you should be reading, ask the careers office, do an internet search and visit a large newsagent. Most trade papers are readily available from large newsagents, but a few are only available on subscription, which you can usually use the internet to sign up for. Serious job hunters should subscribe to a trade paper anyway – you'd kick yourself if you missed a golden opportunity because the local newsagent had sold out of magazines the week the job was advertised.

Internet

Increasingly, jobs are advertised on the internet and you can often send your application in by email, making this very convenient. There are hundreds of internet sites offering current vacancies and you can try to narrow down the ones specialising in the field you want to work in by doing an internet search. Or try some of the sites specifically for graduates, which also often have details of term-time and holiday vacancies. Here are some suggestions to get you going.

Cando – employment and careers advice for disabled students at http://cando.lancs.ac.uk

The Complete Student – a general student site with a jobs section with links to online jobs databases at www.thecompletestudent.co.uk

Graduate Jobs – personalised job vacancies sent by email to subscribers, a jobs database and the option to create your CV online at www.graduate-jobs.com

Gradunet – extensive jobs database, job noticeboards and careers advice at www.gradunet.co.uk

Juiced – a general student site from the *Daily Telegraph* with a careers advice section. It also publishes *Real World* magazine offering advice and information to undergraduates on the range of jobs available and how to get them at www.juiced.co.uk

Milkround Online – a jobs database, career and application advice and updates on employment news at www.milkround.co.uk

Top Graduates – a jobs database, details of graduate recruitment programmes, careers advice and online CV and application forms at www.topgrads.co.uk

Jobcentres

You might feel that you went to university to avoid the Jobcentre, but actually they are really good sources of general careers advice and carry loads of different vacancies which the staff will also help you apply for. You don't have to be registered with the Jobcentre to ask for advice and browse the vacancies and if you do end up signing on while job hunting then make sure you make full use of their services while you are there.

Careers services

Careers services not only offer advice but often carry details of vacancies not advertised elsewhere, particularly some of the fast-track management schemes companies run for graduates. They primarily cater for people aged up to 21 and if that's you then your local careers office is definitely worth a visit.

Recruitment agencies

These can be good, particularly if you want to try out a number of different companies. Many of the vacancies are administrative or secretarial roles for which you may have to be able to type at a certain speed. However, the areas that use recruitment agencies are increasing and now include areas like IT, catering, teaching, etc. Doing a temporary job can be a good way of getting your foot in the door of a company where you can then make yourself indispensable. They may then think of you when vacancies come up. If you have languages then specialist agencies that recruit for translators and interpreters can be a great way of finding a job.

How to hunt those hidden jobs

Over half of vacancies aren't advertised but recruited by word of mouth. This means that it is worth sending your CV off to companies, asking if they have any vacancies. You'll need to do your research thoroughly and make sure that you address it to an appropriate named person (either the head of Personnel or HR or the head of the department you are interested in).

It also means that it is worth trying to arrange work experience (see *What about work experience and placements?*, page 167) to try to get a foot in the door. If money is an issue then try balancing work experience with weekend or evening work but don't do this for too long or you'll end up exhausted and in no fit state to impress future employers.

'I spent some time doing voluntary work for non-governmental organisations (NGOs). It is crucial to have some kind of experience to get a job in the NGO/development field but it is also really helpful for discovering what kind of work you enjoy doing and where you want to go next. And when a job came up at the organisation I was volunteering at I was offered it.'

**Amy North, MSc development studies student,
London School of Economics, University of London**

Get family, friends and acquaintances to keep their eyes open for you. Many job vacancies are advertised internally on company noticeboards or intranet boards. Call them occasionally or email them so they don't forget to look as this can be an excellent way of finding out about jobs. It also means that you have a connection with the company which you can mention at interview.

What if I want to continue studying?

'I'd spent so many years learning all about science that I decided I actually wanted to apply what I had learnt and do science. And any research post always requires you to have done postgraduate education. I'd definitely recommend it. It's very different from a degree – it's more like a job. You are not required to do work in the evenings and you are at liberty to do what you want and when. It's intense but not stressful.'

Jeremy Carlton, PhD biochemistry student,
Bristol University

A growing number of graduates are electing to continue studying. This can be a great way of improving your career prospects and postgraduates usually earn more in their first job than graduates with first degrees. However, postgraduate study costs and you may have difficulty securing enough funding to balance your further study and existing student debt, but if you can then it should be really rewarding. You get to study an area that you are really interested in, often with academics who are renowned in their field.

If you are interested in postgraduate study then speak to your personal tutor or get help finding a course from Prospects (see *Lifesavers*).

What if I want to travel?

'In my final year of my first degree I decided that I wanted to go back to South America, where I had spent my gap year, when I graduated and I had to start thinking about this a while in advance. I needed to set up and/or find projects to work on and get enough funding to go. Often universities have grants for travel or work abroad but the application deadlines can be quite early.'

Amy North, MSc development studies student,
London School of Economics, University of London

If you are tempted by the idea of putting off joining the rat race, and can afford to travel, this could be a good time to do it. It can be difficult to travel once you start working, although some people successfully combine travel with short-term contract jobs or temping jobs through recruitment agencies (see page 183).

However, if you know you would like to look for a career in the future, there are things that you can do while you are travelling to boost your CV and develop skills which you can offer to an employer. Someone who has worked abroad will definitely stand out from the crowd.

You don't have to interrupt your travel either. Depending on where you travel and your experience there will be opportunities to do voluntary work. If you fancy sorting something out in advance then try www.workabroad.co.uk

---

'I have decided that I am not going to look for my ideal job when I leave university. I want to travel so I am going to get a job for a year to save money. I don't know what job I'll go for – whatever is available, so that I can save. I still don't have a clue about what job I ultimately want to do.'

Allan Jones, third-year geography student, Lancaster University

Lifesavers

Your university careers service should be your first port of call for careers advice, help with CV writing and job applications and details of suitable vacancies. You can also get free careers advice and details of graduate vacancies from the careers service local to where you live or study. The service is free to people aged 21 and under. Look in the phone book under 'careers'.

Prospects offers extremely comprehensive advice to students and graduates. It has sections on careers advice, a forum where graduates share their experiences, a careers planning service and details of postgraduate courses round the country. You can send your CV or application form by email to a careers advisor and they will send their comments back. Prospects also has databases of jobs, both for graduates and for students looking for term-time and holiday work, a database of work experience vacancies and a database of careers fairs round the country. www.prospects.ac.uk

Publications

There is a range of publications which have advice on working in a particular area such as publishing, television or management. These tell you more about the industry and provide tips on ways of getting in. Look in large book shops for the area in which you are interested and ask the staff if you can't track down a book on your preferred profession.

There are also many general advice books. Here's a selection to give you an idea of what's available. *Disabled Students 2002* (all the information disabled students need to compete effectively in today's job market) (Hobsons plc, £9.99); *The Graduate Career Book: making the right start for a bright future* by Shirley Jenner (Financial Times Prentice Hall, £18.99); *How to Win as a Final Year Student: essays, exams and employment* by Phil Race (OU Press, £12.99) and *Your First Interview: for students and anyone preparing to enter today's tough job market* by Ron Fry (Career Press, £8.99).

What's what and who's who

Campus: The area where the university teaching buildings are. Many campuses also have student accommodation on site and are completely self-contained centres of student life.

Chancellor: Usually a nominal 'head' of the university, brought out on ceremonial occasions to shake hands and pass on congratulations. To make things more confusing this person is sometimes known as a Visitor.

Dean of students: The person, if one exists in your university, who is responsible for your welfare, both academic and personal.

Department: The part of your university responsible for teaching your course. You can be part of more than one department if you are studying a joint course.

Director of studies: Also known as the head of department, which is much more self-explanatory. Basically, the person responsible for running the department, who may also do some teaching as well.

Executive officers: Elected students there to help sabbatical officers with anything from making posters to representing students' views to the university.

Faculty: An umbrella grouping of related subjects. The Arts faculty carries out administration for the humanities subjects and the Science faculty for the science subjects.

Freshers: The term used to describe all first-year students. You'll get really cheesed off with being called a fresher two terms into your first year by 'mature' second-year students. Ignore them – 12 months from now you'll be doing the same to next year's intake.

Freshers' fairs: Events where the local banks, businesses and students' union clubs and societies all try to persuade you that they are the best thing since sliced bread.

General union meetings: These come under a variety of titles but are basically where all students of the university decide which policies the students' union should adopt and elect the students who are going to run it.

Halls: Halls of residence are buildings where students (usually first years) live.

Lecturer: A member of the department who gives lectures. He or she probably has a specialist field and researches it when not teaching.

Local education authority (LEA): The people to whom you have to apply to be assessed for the proportion of your tuition fees you will be responsible for and how much student loan you are allowed to borrow. In Northern Ireland this department is called the **Education and Library Board (ELB)** and in Scotland it is the **Student Awards Agency for Scotland**. You need to apply each year or you may end up being asked to pay all your tuition fees.

National Union of Students (NUS): The national representative body for students. If your university is a member (and most are) then you will get an NUS card which will entitle you to certain discounts.

Personal tutor: The tutor in your department who's been assigned to look after your welfare. He or she may not be the tutor who teaches you.

Rag: Where students do silly things and have a lot of fun all in the name of charity. It can also be the derogatory, or perhaps affectionate, name for the student newspaper.

Registry: The place where you go to register as a student. It's also the place where you go to pick up your student loan cheque.

Sabbatical officers: Students or finalists elected by the students of the university to take responsibility for running parts of the students' union. They are paid a salary and are very well versed in student issues, having had recent experience of being a student at your university.

Seminars: Group discussions with a lecturer where you have to take your courage in both hands and present a paper.

Student loans: The money you can borrow from the Student Loans Company to cover your living costs. Part of it is means-tested on your income and that of your family and you have to pay it back with interest when you graduate.

Students' unions: Also known as guilds of students, student associations and junior common rooms. The places that provide cheap beer, entertainments, clubs, societies, stationery and food, and can help you with any problem in complete confidence.

Tuition fees: The means-tested amount that you have to pay towards the cost of your course, currently up to £1,100. You have to pay tuition fees for each year of your course (with some limited exceptions). Scottish students studying at Scottish universities don't have to pay tuition fees.

Tutor: The person who teaches you individually or with a small group of other people in a tutorial or seminar.

University: For the purposes of this publication, the term university has been used throughout this book as shorthand for 'university or college/insititute of higher education'.

Vice-chancellor: If you have a VC then he or she will be the big boss who does all the hard work and is responsible for running the university. It gets confusing because these people are also known as Principals, Directors and Deans – it depends on what basis your university was set up.

Vice-principal: Deputy to the VC.

Welfare officer: The sabbatical officer and/or member of staff who is responsible for the welfare of all the students at the university. Very helpful, totally unshockable people who have seen it all before. The first point of contact for any difficulties you have while at university.

The Student Helpbook series

Jobs and Careers after A Levels and equivalent advanced level qualifications

Opportunities for students leaving school or college at 18
£9.99   ISBN: 1 902876 15 6

NEW EDITION
A Year Off... A Year On?

All the information and advice you need on how to make the most of your time out between courses or jobs
£10.99   ISBN: 1 902876 32 6

NEW EDITION
CVs and Applications

For anyone who is applying for a job or college place
£10.99   ISBN: 1 902876 31 8

NEW EDITION
Excel at Interviews

New edition of this highly successful title, invaluable reading for students and jobhunters
£10.99   ISBN: 1 90287630 X

Careers with a Science Degree

Compulsory reading for anyone considering science at degree level
£9.99   ISBN: 1 873408 93 5

Careers with an Arts Degree

Compulsory reading for anyone considering arts at degree level
£9.99   ISBN: 1 873408 92 7

For further details please contact:

Customer Services, Lifetime Careers Publishing, 7 Ascot Court,
White Horse Business Park, Trowbridge, BA14 0XA
Tel: 01225 716023; Fax: 01225 716025
Email: sales@wiltshire.lifetime-careers.co.uk